PENGUIN BOOKS

HOW TO WATCH TV NEWS

Neil Postman (1931–2003) was chairman of the Department of Communication Arts at New York University and founder of its program in media ecology. He wrote nineteen books, including *Amusing Ourselves to Death* and *Technopoly*. In 1986, he won the George Orwell Award for clarity in language.

Steve Powers is a journalist with more than forty-five years' experience in radio and television news, including as a newscaster for the *New York Times* radio network, an anchor/reporter for Fox Television News in New York, a correspondent for the ABC Information Radio Network, and the host of a top-rated morning talk show. He has received an Emmy, a Clio, and a New York Press Club Deadline Award. Powers earned his Ph.D. in media studies from New York University in 1987 and was an associate professor of communications at St. John's University in New York.

HOW TO
WATCH
TV NEWS

Neil Postman
and Steve Powers

With New and Updated Material
by Steve Powers

PENGUIN BOOKS

PENGUIN BOOKS

Published by the Penguin Group

Penguin Group (USA) Inc., 375 Hudson Street, New York, New York 10014, U.S.A.
Penguin Group (Canada), 90 Eglinton Avenue East, Suite 700, Toronto, Ontario,
Canada M4P 2Y3 (a division of Pearson Penguin Canada Inc.)
Penguin Books Ltd, 80 Strand, London WC2R 0RL, England
Penguin Ireland, 25 St Stephen's Green, Dublin 2, Ireland
(a division of Penguin Books Ltd)
Penguin Group (Australia), 250 Camberwell Road, Camberwell, Victoria 3124,
Australia (a division of Pearson Australia Group Pty Ltd)
Penguin Books India Pvt Ltd, 11 Community Centre, Panchsheel Park,
New Delhi - 110 017, India
Penguin Group (NZ), 67 Apollo Drive, Rosedale, North Shore 0632, New Zealand
(a division of Pearson New Zealand Ltd)
Penguin Books (South Africa) (Pty) Ltd, 24 Sturdee Avenue, Rosebank,
Johannesburg 2196, South Africa

Penguin Books Ltd, Registered Offices:
80 Strand, London WC2R 0RL, England

First published in Penguin Books 1992
This revised edition published 2008

10 9 8 7 6 5 4 3 2 1

Copyright © Neil Postman and Steve Powers, 1992
Copyright © Steve Powers, 2008
All rights reserved

LIBRARY OF CONGRESS CATALOGING IN PUBLICATION DATA
Postman, Neil.
How to watch TV news/Neil Postman and Steve Powers ; with new and updated
materials by Steve Powers.—Rev. ed.
p.   cm.
Includes index.
ISBN 978-0-14-311377-5
1. Television broadcasting of news—United States—Social aspects. 2. Television
broadcasting of news—United States—Psychological aspects. 3. Content analysis
(Communication) I. Powers, Steve, Ph. D. II. Title.
PN4888.T4P58 2008
070.4'3—dc22   2008015156

Printed in the United States of America
Set in Aldus with Agenda and Helvetica
Designed by Sabrina Bowers

Author's Note

I WAS FORTUNATE TO HAVE a preeminent scholar and prescient thinker, Neil Postman, as both my teacher and coauthor for the original edition of How to Watch TV News. Unfortunately, he died on October 5, 2003, before this revision of the book.

His forward thinking, insights, and seminal work on the original manuscript remain largely intact; my mentor's teachings permeate each page. I miss his counsel, original thoughts, sense of humor, and friendship.

STEVE POWERS
NOVEMBER 2007

Contents

Preface

THIS BOOK WAS WRITTEN by two men with different kinds of knowledge about television but with similar points of view. Without this similarity we would not have been of interest to each other. Without the difference we probably would not be of interest to the reader. One of us, Neil Postman, was an academic who wrote books on the effects of the media and, especially, on how television has altered various forms of social life. Although he once had a television show of his own (forty-eight half-hour programs under the aegis of *Sunrise Semester*), he felt he was not skilled in the art of using television as a medium of communication. The other, Steve Powers, is a television/radio journalist who has done thousands of news stories, interviews, and broadcasts over a forty-five-year career. He has a Ph.D. in media studies but spent most of his professional life as a practitioner of both radio and television journalism. Postman's head was filled with theories, historical knowledge, and visions of what an awesome technology like television ought to do for a culture. Powers's head is filled with practical knowledge of what television, in fact, does, how it does it, and what it might do. We came to the conclusion some years ago that what television news says it is presenting and what it actually delivers are two different things. We concluded that a tidy and truthful book on how people should prepare themselves to interpret a television news show might be useful. The book at hand is the result.

Before saying anything else of the matter, we need to remark that anyone who is not an avid reader of newspapers, magazines, and books is by definition unprepared to watch television news shows, and will always be. This point has been made many times with special force by such television journalists as Walter Cronkite, Bill Moyers, and Robert MacNeil. Anyone who relies exclusively on television for his or her knowledge of the world is making a serious mistake. Just as television can show things about the world that cannot be experienced through print, print can reveal complexities and facts that are not possible to show on television. Therefore, those who have not read about the world are limited in their capacity to understand what they see on television. As an example, consider television's presentation of the uprising by Chinese students in Tiananmen Square. Anyone who watched diligently will never forget the image of a solitary student standing in front of a tank, obstructing it from proceeding. Mao Tse-tung preached that power begins behind the barrel of a gun. But this image, as media critic Jay Rosen once remarked, seemed to suggest that power also comes to those who *face* the barrel of a gun, provided that a camera catches them in the act and that the image is witnessed by a vast audience. It was television journalism at its best. But if that were all someone knew about the student uprising, it wouldn't be very much. One would have to know something about who rules China, and where those rulers came from, and by what authority or ideology they claim to rule, and how the students interpreted the meaning of freedom and democracy. These are complex matters that are beyond the scope of simple television newscasts and must be learned through extensive reading of newspapers and books.

And so, the first lesson we have to teach is that preparation for watching television news begins with the preparation of one's mind through extensive reading. This lesson is of sufficient importance that we have seen fit to include it in our preface. Having made this essential point, we will now turn our attention to all the others.

Acknowledgments

WE WISH TO ACKNOWLEDGE the assistance of some of the people who generously provided us with their time and expertise: Professor Jay Rosen of New York University, especially for his help on chapter 8; Professor Paul Thaler of Mercy College for his research on television in the courtroom and for even allowing us to use a few of his own words; Dr. Eva Berger of Tel Aviv University for providing a continuous flow of constructive criticism; Karen Anderson and Alexis Washam, the editors of this edition, whose sensitivity and sharp eyes and minds kept the material and form on track; Sheri Powers, whose experience in television news gave us insights to help guide us; Dr. Harry Royson for his inspiration; Shelley Postman and Andrew Postman for their encouragement; Janet Sternberg of New York University for her editorial skills and especially for her speedy and creative use of a word processor; Stan Moger of SFM Entertainment for sharing his astute television business acumen; and Jeff Baker and John Gonzalez of WNBC-TV for their cutting-edge technical know-how and their willingness to share it.

CHAPTER 1

Are You Watching Television, or Is Television Watching You?

CHANCES ARE YOU HAVE at least one television set in your home that is used by most members of your family. Surveys of viewing patterns show that in an average household the television set is on about eight hours and fourteen minutes a day. According to Nielsen Media Research, the average amount of television watched by individual viewers is currently a record four hours and thirty-five minutes a day. Nowadays, with the availability of cable, satellite, and the Internet, there are more programs than we have time to watch, especially with the various methods of capturing and viewing programs, such as TiVos, DVRs, VCRs, and portable media players. There are networks that carry only comedy or news or music or courtroom proceedings or financial information or weather or programs for babies and pets. There are even channels for shopping addicts who can't get enough buying done during regular hours at their favorite stores. Insomniacs know "when sleep is stopping . . . you can always go shopping." The 112.8 million households in the United States with television have access to a constant stream of tempting programs to divert them every waking hour of the day. And, of course, there is the tremendous number of movies and other shows that can be downloaded, rented, or traded among aficionados. All these programs are vying for your attention and time. Each show, series, channel, and network is waving its electronic billboard at you, trying to grab your attention; in effect, saying, "Watch me, watch me." But your time is limited and valuable so you choose the programs you want to watch, and if you have a recording device, you even choose when you want to watch them.

With such an awesome technology at our beck and call, we tend to think of television as just another appliance. Put it on when you want to; turn it off when you're through. Since you control it, you think that television is a one-way street: that you are using it, and it is not using you. But that is simply not the case. It may not be able to see you eating snacks in your living room, but television is still keeping an eye on you in different ways. The fact of the matter is that television not only delivers programs to your home, but, more important to the advertising community, it also delivers you to a sponsor.

Advertisers and suppliers of programs spend a fortune slicing, dicing, chopping, and crunching numbers that tell them what you are watching, along with every other bit of information about you they can get. They are not playing *Jeopardy!* The kind of knowledge the advertisers seek gives them power, and the more they know about you, the easier it is to sell you something. Developers of interactive television boast that in the future they will be able to send specific commercials to their subscribers based on the household's demographic composition. Theoretically, commercials for sneakers can be programmed to families with children who play basketball, while another commercial, perhaps for prescription drugs, can be sent to another family, composed of older people. That's in the future: in effect, custom-tailored sales pitches.

But right now, advertisers have to rely on attracting a large-enough audience to their programs to deliver their messages. In fact, the reason popular TV series get on the air and stay there is that they can deliver the right audience for a sponsor, an audience that sees commercials and buys products or ideas. There is no escaping that fact: the whole point of television in America is to get you to watch so that programmers, performers, and others can rake in the money. Published reports say Merv Griffin, who originated the program *Wheel of Fortune*, sold his company to Coca-Cola for $250 million, which in turn sold it to the Sony Corporation for even more. It has been reported in *Forbes* magazine that Oprah Winfrey has an estimated annual income of $260 million. *Forbes* also reported that Jerry Seinfeld received $267 million during 1998, making him the highest-earning celebrity that year. He reportedly turned down $5 million per episode (for twenty-two episodes) to continue *Seinfeld* beyond its final season. Even though the show ended production in May 1998, it still generates $60 million a year through syndication—more revenue than most current shows.

All of which is to say that American television producers have been enormously successful in attracting large audiences. Their programs have been so popular that they threaten to undermine the TV systems of other countries throughout the world. For example, several countries, including Canada and Australia, limit the number of American TV programs on the air so that more time can be given to their own programs, emphasizing their own cultural values. This is not easy to do since American programs, when in direct competition with local shows, consistently draw audiences away from homegrown products and create a demand for more American programs.

It might look like American TV producers are having everything their own way. Not so. The cost of producing sitcoms and other forms of popular entertainment has been growing. According to *Forbes*, an average half hour of sitcom costs $1.3 million. The popular TV show *Everybody Loves Raymond* paid its star, Ray Romano, $2 million per episode. Kelsey Grammer took home $1.6 million for each *Frasier*. Tim Allen got $1.25 million for *Home Improvement*, and the six cast members of *Friends*, $1 million each per episode. And that doesn't count additional production costs. Scripted TV shows cost between $2 million and $3 million an hour. Reality shows generally cost $1 million to $3 million to produce. Producers claim they have to sell their programs to the networks, then syndicate them to make a profit. And while costs have been increasing, the audience for individual shows has declined as viewers find more and different channels and recordings to watch. It's no secret that news programs cost a lot less to produce than slick Hollywood dramas and laugh-track comedies. An hour-long news program, such as the CBS show *48 Hours*, costs $500,000 or less. Compare that to an hour of so-called entertainment programming, with fancy production values, at well more than twice the cost, and you will know why the networks and other producers are interested in news programs.

With the cost of news being relatively inexpensive, there is more of it being presented on television now than ever before. Not too long ago, television news programs were money-losing products limited to a half hour each day and the Sunday-morning "public affairs" ghetto. In 1969, the year American astronauts walked on the moon, the three major network evening newscasts were watched in 50 percent of American homes. The ratings have fallen 62 percent since that peak, and the audience is getting older and older. The average

age of the person who watches the news on any of the three networks is now sixty. The news is, however, still profitable for television networks. There are all-news cable channels, all-business news channels, all-sports news channels, entertainment news shows, Spanish-language news shows, special television news programs for children beamed into classrooms, and a plethora of other network and syndicated news shows. Playing the numbers, there are *48 Hours*, *60 Minutes*, and *20/20*. There are tabloid news shows and programs featuring dramatic re-creations. Every night an estimated 27 million people watch the news on the major networks, and millions watch cable and local news coverage. Derek Blaine, a senior analyst at SNL Kagan, estimates that in 2006 CNN, Fox News Channel, and MSNBC collectively produced $698.7 million in cash flow with a total average prime-time audience of over 2.8 million. And then there are early-morning shows (watched by about 12.5 million viewers) and late-night news programs (3.5 million people watch *Nightline* alone). Morning news shows bring in some $1 billion in ad revenue each year.

Today attracts an average of 6.1 million predominantly female viewers daily. In January 2008, an average of 4.9 million viewers tuned into *Good Morning America* every day, and over at CBS, *The Early Show* averages 2.8 million. All of this translates into dollars. An NBC executive told the *New York Times* that *Today* earns $500 million a year for the network. *Good Morning America* earns $300 million to $400 million, and *The Early Show* is reaching for $200 million. Continuing to milk the cash cow, NBC added a fourth hour to *Today* in September 2007. Networks are making heavy profits from news, and on-air talent is being paid more than ever to communicate to the public.

More than just profitable, the news audience is a highly desirable one. People who watch news tend to be more attentive to what is on the screen. They tend to be better educated, albeit older, and have more money to spend than the audiences for other shows. They are, therefore, a prime target for advertisers trying to reach an affluent market. To reach that audience, sponsors are willing to pour money into well-produced commercials. These spots are often longer than most news stories and certainly cost more to produce. The commercials are fast paced, exciting, and colorful and, as a result, influence the way the news stories around them are produced. Propelled by the energy of the "Madison Avenue shuffle," the whole news program takes on a rhythm and pace designed to hold interest and build viewership. More viewers, higher ratings, more advertising dollars, more profit, more similar programs to try to attract more viewers—ad infinitum.

While public service does play a role in deciding what news programs get on the air, the main factor is profit. In fact, while news operations used to be considered a nonprofit public service, in the new economics, news departments and programs are expected to make money, and they do. CBS News spends about $500 million annually, and ABC and NBC each spend about $600 million. It's estimated that in 2006 ABC made just under $100 million from commercials aired on the news alone. NBC News earns about $270 million; CBS, a bit more. Executives at ABC have been quoted as saying that while being number one in the ratings used to be worth an additional $30 million, it is no longer true. The new standard of success, ABC says, is how the demographic of the audience breaks down into age groups, with younger viewers favored by advertisers.

Of course, some news professionals believe that news departments dedicated to good, solid journalism will bring credibility to the whole broadcast network or local station and that therefore profit should come second to educating the public for the common good. But news professionals aren't usually as powerful as accountants. The idea is to make as much money as possible from news departments, sometimes to the detriment of truth and journalism.

Every broadcaster tries to determine how much programs are worth to the advertiser. But since they cannot go around to every home to find out what everyone is watching, broadcasters depend on ratings systems to measure audiences. Companies that do the surveys, such as Nielsen and Arbitron, use so-called scientific samples to find out how many people are watching each show. Nielsen not only measures how many people are watching each show but, since January 2006, estimates how many watch the show after recording it on a DVR (digital video recorder). In 2007, it started reporting the average audience for the commercials in a given show, including commercials seen, and not fast-forwarded, via DVR.

In the Nielsen Media Research measurement system, a rating point represents 1,128,000 households or 1 percent of the nation's estimated 112.8 million TV homes (homes with television sets). This share is the percentage of television sets being used, tuned to a given show. In September 2007, Nielsen announced that by 2011 it would be tripling the size of its National People Meter television ratings sample. To project national ratings, Nielsen now takes viewing information from twelve thousand U.S. households and thirty-five thousand people. That sample will increase to thirty-seven thousand homes and one hundred thousand people. Meanwhile, a large group of viewers may consist of a few thousand people. From time to time the sample may be exactly representational, but not always—not by a long shot. In one case, a blind fan living in the Bridgeport, Connecticut, area represented a hundred thousand people. He enjoyed listening to television; the shows with the most interesting soundtrack got his vote.

Rating companies do not simply count the viewers of a particular show. As we mentioned earlier, they slice, dice, chop, and crunch the viewer information, then report to advertisers who pay them for these statistics. They try to know the age of those watching a specific show, their income, their level of education, what kinds of cars they own, what appliances they've bought, their eating habits, etc. The answers are produced from questions a sample of viewers answers either over the phone or in writing, from logs that the viewers fill out, and from various electronic devices that automatically register the programs being watched and even "read" the number of people in the room. Nielsen has announced that it will be making available minute-by-minute audience data for all national programming sources. If a person who is being sampled turns on the TV set for even two seconds, she is being counted as watching for a full minute. And while the minute-by-minute information is valuable to the advertiser to measure commercial viewing, imagine its potential effect on news producers. ABC News anchor Charles Gibson says he does not look at the ratings, so they do not influence the content of the newscasts. But one would think that if a story—say Anna Nicole Smith's death—drew big ratings, producers would be tempted to try to run more stories related to it, to the detriment of less-popular and more important news. In fact, when pop star Britney Spears became the paparazzi's favorite target, an Associated Press Los Angeles assistant bureau chief sent a memo to his reporters that said "Now and for the foreseeable future, virtually everything involving Britney Spears is a big deal."

The prevalence of recording devices like TiVo (in 14 percent of American households in 2007) has led to three published versions of Nielsen's program ratings: how many people watch a program when it is originally broadcast, how many watch it within one day, and how many within a week. Advertisers want to know how many people watch the commercials without fast-forwarding them and how many have their sets on during commercials. In addition, information about what programs you watch can be monitored digitally by satellite and cable and devices like TiVo. TiVo sells data on how its 4.4 million users watch commercials or skip them, information based on an analysis of the second-by-second viewing patterns of a nightly sample of twenty thousand TiVo users.

What all this means is that while you are watching the TV set, you are being statistically watched, and very carefully, by managers, accountants, and businesspeople. They argue that they must know who you are to mirror your interests and give you what you want. And to pay for it, they must run commercials. They also point out that other news media—newspapers, for example—are moneymaking enterprises and rely on advertising just as heavily as does television. These arguments make perfect sense in a free-enterprise business with no social responsibility. But we would stress that broadcasting is not just another business enterprise. Broadcasting is a government-licensed activity using publicly owned airwaves and facilities, and therefore broadcasters have an obligation not only to make money but to enlighten the public by supplying news and programs of serious content, for all segments of the population. To this the TV establishment replies that television is the most democratic institution in America. Every week a plebiscite of sorts is held to determine which programs are popular and which are not. The popular ones stay, the others go. This proves, the accountants say, that the programs give the public what it wants.

Serious journalists and social critics have an answer, at least as far as news is concerned. It is this: when providing entertainment, the public's preferences must be paramount. But news is different. There are things the public must know whether or not they "like" it. To understand what is happening in the world, and what it means, requires knowledge of historical, political, and social contexts. It is the task of journalists to provide people with such knowledge. News is not entertainment. It is a necessity in a democratic society. Therefore, TV news must give people what they *need* along with what they *want*. The solution is to present news in a form that will compel the attention of a large audience without subverting the goal of informing the public. But as things stand now, it is essential that any viewer understand the following when turning on a TV news show:

1. American television is an unsleeping money machine.
2. While journalists pursue newsworthy events, business-oriented management often makes decisions based on business considerations.
3. Many decisions about the form and content of news programs are made on the basis of information about the viewer, the purpose of which is to keep viewers watching so that they will be exposed to commercials.

This is, obviously, not all that can be said about news. If it were, we could end our book here. But anything else that can, and will, be said must be understood within the framework of TV news as a *commercial* enterprise.

CHAPTER 2

What Is News?

ALL THIS TALK ABOUT news, but what is it? We turn to this question because unless a television viewer has considered it, he or she is in danger of too easily accepting someone else's definition: for example, one supplied by the news director of a television station or, even worse, imposed by important advertisers. The question, in any case, is not a simple one, and it is even possible that many journalists and advertisers have not thought deeply about it.

A simplistic definition of news can be drawn by paraphrasing Justice Oliver Wendell Holmes's famous definition of the law. The law, Holmes said, is what the courts say it is. Nothing more. Nothing less. In similar fashion, we might say that the news is what news directors and journalists say it is. In other words, when you turn on your television set to watch a network or local news show, whatever is on is, by definition, the news. But if we were to take that approach, on what basis could we say that we haven't been told enough? Or that a story should have been covered but wasn't? Or that too many stories of a certain type were included? Or that a reporter gave a flagrantly biased account?

If objections of this kind are raised by viewers, they must have some conception of the news that the news show has not fulfilled. Most people, in fact, do have such a conception, although they are not always fully conscious of what it is. When people are asked, "What is the news?" the most frequent answer is that the news is "what happened that day." This is a rather silly answer since even those who give it can easily be made to see that an uncountable number of things happen during the course of a day, including your breakfast, that could hardly be classified as news by any definition. In modifying their answer, most will add that the news is "important and interesting events that happened that day." This helps a little but leaves open the question of what is "important and interesting" and how that is decided. Embedded somewhere in one's understanding of the phrase "important and interesting events" is one's definition of the news.

Of course, some people will say that the question of what is important and interesting is not in the least problematic. What the president says or does is important; wars are important, and so are rebellions, employment figures, elections, and appointments to the Supreme Court. Really? We doubt that even the president believes everything he says is important (take, for example, the elder president Bush's remark that he doesn't like broccoli). There are, as we write, more than fifteen to twenty wars and rebellions going on in the world. Not even the *New York Times*, which claims to be the "newspaper of public record," reports on all, or even most, of them. Are elections important? Maybe. But we doubt you're too interested in the election in Iowa's Third Congressional District, unless you happen to live there. Some readers will remember the famous comedy routine "The Two Thousand Year Old Man" by Carl Reiner and Mel Brooks. Upon being asked what he believed to be the greatest invention of humankind during his life span, the old man replied unhesitatingly, "Saran Wrap." Now, there is a great deal to be said for Saran Wrap. We suspect that in the long run it may prove more useful to the well-being of most of us than a number of inventions daily given widespread publicity in the news media. Yet it is fair to say that almost no one except its manufacturer knows the date of Saran Wrap's invention or even cares much to know. Saran Wrap is not news. The latest Hollywood star charged with DUI is. Or so some people believe.

On the day Marilyn Monroe committed suicide, so did many other people, some of whom may have had reasons as engrossing as, and perhaps more significant than, Miss Monroe's. But we shall never know about those people or their reasons; the journalists at CBS and NBC and the *New York Times* simply took no notice of them. Several people, we are sure, also committed suicide on the day in 2006 when the St. Louis Cardinals won the World Series. We shall never learn about those people either, however instructive or interesting their stories may have been.

What we are driving at is this: "importance" is a judgment people make. Of course, some events—the assassination of a president, an earthquake, etc.—have near-universal interest and consequences. But most news does not inhere in the event. An event *becomes* news. And it becomes news because it is selected for notice out of the buzzing, booming confusion around us. This may seem a fairly obvious point, but keep in mind that many people believe the news is always "out there" waiting to be gathered or collected. In fact, the news is more often *made* than gathered. And it is made on the basis of what the journalist thinks important or what the journalist thinks the audience thinks is important or interesting.

In September 2007, a study by the Project for Excellence in Journalism showed that people who went online for their news gravitated toward topics different from those offered by traditional news outlets. Many of the stories selected by online users did not even appear anywhere among the top stories in the mainstream media. The study found that on Yahoo! News, even when choosing from a limited list of stories Yahoo! editors had selected, users' top stories only rarely matched those picked by the news professionals. The survey concluded, "In short, the user-news agenda, at least in this one-week snapshot, was more diverse, yet also more fragmented and transitory than that of the mainstream news media." In the week reviewed "when the mainstream press was focused on Iraq and the debate over immigration, the three leading user-news sites—reddit.com, Digg, and del.icio. us—were focused on stories like the release of Apple's new iPhone and that Nintendo had surpassed Sony in net worth."

It can get pretty complicated. Is a story about a killing in Northern Ireland more important than one about a killing in Morocco? The journalist might not think so, but the audience might. Which story will become the news? And once selected, what point of view and details are to be included? After all, once a journalist has chosen an event to be news, he or she must also choose what about it is worth seeing, is worth neglecting, and is worth remembering or forgetting. This is simply another way of saying that every news story is a reflection of the reporter who tells the story. The reporter's previous assumptions about what is "out there" edit what he or she thinks is there. For example, many journalists believe that the intifada in the Middle East is newsworthy. Let us suppose that a fourteen-year-old Palestinian boy hurls a Molotov cocktail at two eighteen-year-old Israeli soldiers. The explosion knocks one of the soldiers down and damages his left eye. The other soldier, terrified, fires a shot that kills the Palestinian instantly. The injured soldier eventually loses his sight in the damaged eye. What details should be included in reporting this event? Is the age of the Palestinian relevant? Are the ages of the Israeli soldiers relevant? Is the injury to the soldier relevant? Was the act of the Palestinian provoked by the mere presence of the Israeli soldiers? Was the act therefore justified? Is shooting justified? Is the state of mind of the shooter relevant?

The answers to all these questions, as well as to other questions about the event, depend entirely on the point of view of the journalist. You might think this an exaggeration, that reporters, irrespective of their assumptions, can at least get the facts straight. But what are facts? In A. J. Liebling's book *The Press,* he gives a classic example of the problematic nature of "facts." On the same day, some years ago, both the *Wall Street Journal* and the now-defunct *World-Telegram and Sun* featured a story about the streets of Moscow. Here is what the *Wall Street Journal* reporter wrote:

> The streets of central Moscow are, as the guidebooks say, clean and neat; so is the famed subway. They are so because of an army of women with brooms, pans, and carts who thus earn their 35 rubles a month in lieu of "relief"; in all Moscow we never saw a mechanical street sweeper.

Here is what the *World-Telegram and Sun* reporter wrote:

> Four years ago [in Moscow] women by the hundreds swept big city streets. Now you rarely see more than a dozen. The streets are kept clean with giant brushing and sprinkling machines.

Well, which is it? Can a dozen women look like an army? Are there giant machines cleaning the streets of Moscow or not? How can two trained journalists see events so differently? Well, one of them worked for the *Wall Street Journal*, and when these stories were written, it was the policy of the *Journal* to highlight the contrast between the primitive Russian economy and the sophisticated American economy (it still is). Does this mean the *Journal* reporter was lying? Unlikely. Each of our senses is a remarkably astute censor. For example, in a journalism class on reporting at New York University, the professor arranged for a man to burst into a class unannounced. The man shouted gibberish at the professor, waving his arms in a threatening way. Most students dove for cover, and a few stood up protectively as the man completed his unintelligible tirade and then ran out of the room.

When asked to write down what they heard and saw, the class had varying answers. Some described the man as having a mustache, others a full beard. Some said his shirt was green, others red. His pants were brown, or black, and so on. Some heard him say he was jealous of the professor's relationship with his wife, another heard the man accuse the professor of stealing something from him. All those conflicting descriptions; all those ears hearing the same thing, all those eyes observing the same scene! We see what we expect to see. Often, we focus on what we are paid to see. And those who pay us to see usually expect us to accept their notions not only of what is important but of what details are important.

That fact poses some difficult problems for those of us trying to make sense of the news we are given. One of those problems is indicated by a proposal, made years ago, by the great French writer Albert Camus. Camus wished to establish "a control newspaper." The paper would come out one hour after all the others and would contain estimates of the percentage of truth in each of the stories. In Camus's words (quoted in Liebling's *The Press*): "We'd have complete dossiers on the interests, policies, and idiosyncrasies of the owners. Then we'd have a dossier on every journalist in the world. The interests, prejudices, and quirks of the owner would equal Z. The prejudices, quirks, and private interests of the journalist Y. Z times Y would give you X, the probable amount of truth in the story."

Camus was either a reckless mathematician or else he simply neglected to say why and how multiplying Z and Y would tell us what we need to know. (Why not add or divide them?) Nor did he discuss the problem of how to estimate the reliability of those doing the estimating. In any case, Camus died before he had a chance to publish such a newspaper, leaving each one of us to be our own "control" center. Nonetheless, we can't help thinking about how Camus's idea might be applied to television. Imagine how informative it would be if there were a five-minute television program that went on immediately after each television news show. The host might say something like this: "To begin with, this station is owned by Gary Farnsworth, who is also the president of Bontel Limited, the principal stockholder in which is the sultan of Bahrain. Bontel Limited owns three Japanese electronics companies, two oil companies, the entire country of Burkina Faso, and the western part of Romania. The anchorman on the television show earns $800,000 a year; his portfolio includes holdings in a major computer firm. He has a bachelor's degree in journalism from the University of Arkansas but was a C-plus student, has never taken a course in political science, and speaks no language other than English. Last year, he read only two books: a biography of Angelina Jolie and a book of popular psychology called *Why Am I So Depressed?* The reporter who covered the story on Iraq speaks Arabic, has a degree in international relations, and had a Neiman Fellowship at Harvard University."

We think this kind of information would be helpful to a viewer, although not for the same reason Camus did. Such information would not give an estimate of the "truth probability" of stories, but it would suggest possible patterns of influence reflected in the news. After all, what is important to a person whose boss owns several oil companies might not be important to a person who doesn't even have a boss, who is unemployed. Similarly, the perceptions of a reporter who does not know the language of the people he or she reports on will probably be different from those of a reporter who knows the language well.

What we are saying is that to answer the question "What is news?" a viewer must know something about the political beliefs and economic situation of those who provide the news. The viewer is then in a better position to know why certain events are considered important by those in charge of television news and may compare those judgments with his or her own. This would have been helpful, for example, in May 2007 when "Breaking News" flashed on the bottom of the screen following a Rangers play-off game in Madison Square Garden. What was the breathtaking breaking news? We quote, "Tony Bennett will be appearing at Radio City Music Hall in September." It would have helped to know that MSG cable is owned by Cablevision and—surprise—that Cablevision also owns Radio City.

Consider that General Electric lists these media companies it owns:

Bravo, CNBC, Focus Features, international channels, MSNBC (with Microsoft), mun2, NBC Entertainment, NBC News, NBC television network, NBC Universal Cable, NBC Universal Sports & Olympics, NBC Universal International Television Distribution, NBC Universal Television Studio, Paxson, Sci Fi, ShopNBC, Telemundo, TRIO, Universal Parks & Resorts, Universal Pictures, Universal Studios Home Entertainment, and the USA Network.

GE also owns part of:

A&E cable, American Movie Classics, Biography, Court TV, The History Channel, National Geographic Worldwide, among others.

Beyond media, GE Advanced Materials, makes:

LNP Engineering Plastics, plastics, polymershapes, quartz, silicones, specialty film and sheets.

GE's Consumer and Industrial division makes:

automotive, commercial lighting, electrical distribution, and entertainment products.

GE has a hand in energy, dealing in:

air-cooled heat exchangers, boiler management products, centrifugal pumps, combined cycle, compressors, electrical test equipment, environmental products, gas turbines, generators, GIS and platform software, hydropower and water control, nuclear plants and instrumentation, oil exploration systems and sensors, plant performance software, radiation monitors, reactors and steam condensers, reciprocating gas engines, reducing and metering systems, SCADA/EMS/DMS software, steam turbines, substation automation products, substation monitoring and diagnostics, telecommunications software, turbine control systems, turboexpanders, utility software, valves, and wind turbines.

GE is involved in healthcare, including

biomedical engineering, cardiology, clinical information systems, emergency department, gastrointestinal center, intensive and critical care units, obstetrics, oncology, orthopedics and sports medicine, radiology, surgery and perioperative, wireless clinical communications networks, and a women's health center.

GE's involvement with infrastructure includes

sensing, security, water, GE Fanuc Automation.

GE has interests in insurance solutions:

Global Life & Health, Global Property & Casualty, and GE Commercial Insurance.

GE Transportation is involved in:

commercial engines, corporate aviation, drilling, freight rail, marine aviation, marine and stationary, military aviation, mining, and passenger rail.

Media educator Ben Bagdikian says that even "though today's media reach more Americans than ever before, they are controlled by the smallest number of owners than ever before . . . in 1983, there were fifty dominant media corporations, today there are five." Indeed, Senator Ernest "Fritz" Hollings (D-SC) and Senator Ted Stevens (R-AK), both members of the Commerce Committee, complained that the Federal Communications Commission (FCC) is "allowing the self-interest of a few media titans to trump the public's interest in protecting a diverse marketplace of ideas." Beside the problem on concentrated ownership, Hollings said, "Already the top five programmers—Viacom/CBS, Disney/ABC, NBC, Time Warner and News Corp./Fox—now control 75 percent of prime-time programming and are soon projected to increase their share to 85 percent."

There is evidence that the media concentration is having an effect on local news coverage. A former lawyer at the FCC claims the commission ordered its staff to destroy all copies of a draft study that suggested greater concentration of media ownership would hurt local TV news coverage. The report, written in 2004, came to light during the Senate confirmation hearing for FCC chairman Kevin Martin.

And here's another problem: As we have implied, even oil magnates and poorly prepared journalists do not consult, exclusively, their own interests in selecting the "truths" they will tell. Since they want people to watch their shows, they also try to determine what audiences think is important and interesting. There is, in fact, a point of view that argues against journalists' imposing their own sense of significance on an audience. In this view, television news should consist only of those events that would interest the audience. The journalists must keep their own opinions to themselves. The response to this is that many viewers depend on journalists to advise them of what is important. Besides, even if journalists were mere followers of public interest, not all members of the audience agree on what they wish to know. For example, we do not happen to think that Larry King's adventures in marriage are of any importance to anyone but him and Frada Miller, Alene Akins, Mickey Sutphin, Sharon Lepore, Julie Alexander, and Shawn Southwick. Nor are Jennifer Lopez's marriages to Cris Judd, Ojani Noa, Marc Anthony and her engagement to Ben Affleck important news. Why would anyone care about the latest party Paris Hilton attended and how much she had to drink and who spilled what on whom? What's our point? A viewer must not only know what he or she thinks is significant but what others believe is significant as well.

It is a matter to be seriously considered. You may conclude, for example, that other people do not have a profound conception of what is significant. You may even be contemptuous of the tastes or interests of others. Or, you may share your sense of significance with the majority of people. It is not our purpose here to question what you or anyone else may regard as a significant event. We are, however, saying that in considering the question "What is news?" the viewer must always take into account his or her relationship to a larger audience. Television is a mass medium, which means that a television news show is not intended for you alone. It is public communication, and the viewer needs to have some knowledge and opinions about "the public." It is a common complaint of individuals that television news rarely includes stories about some part of the world in which those individuals have some special interest. We know a man, for example, who emigrated from Switzerland thirty years ago. He is an American citizen but retains a lively interest in his native land. "Why," he asked us, "are there never any stories about Switzerland?" "Because," we had to reply, "no one but you and a few others have any interest in Switzerland." "That's too bad," he replied. "Switzerland is an interesting country." We agree. But most Americans have not been to Switzerland, probably believe that not much happens in Switzerland, do not have many relatives in Switzerland, and would much rather know about what some English lord has to say about the world's economy than what a Swiss banker thinks. Maybe they are right, maybe not. Judging the public mind is always risky.

And this leads to another difficulty in answering the question "What is news?" Some might agree with us that Paris Hilton's adventures do not constitute significant events but also think that they ought to be included in a news show precisely for that reason. Her experiences, they may say, are amusing or diverting, certainly engrossing. In other words, the purpose of news should be to give people pleasure, at least to the extent that it takes their minds off their own troubles. We have heard people say that getting through the day is difficult enough: filled with tension, anxiety, and often disappointment. When they turn on the news, they want relief, not aggravation. It is also said that whether entertaining or not, stories about the lives of celebrities should be included because they are instructive; they reveal a great deal about our society: its mores, values, ideals. Mark Twain once remarked that news is history in its first and best form. The American poet Ezra Pound added an interesting idea to that. He defined literature as news that *stays* news. Among other things, Pound meant that the stuff of literature originates not in stories about the World Bank or an armistice agreement but in those simple, repeatable tales that reflect the pain, confusion, or exaltations that are constant in human experience and touch us at the deepest levels. For example, consider the death of Princess Diana. Who was Diana to you or you to Diana that you should have been told so much about her when she died? Here is a possible answer: Diana Spencer was a beautiful commoner who became a princess and involved in the world. Suddenly, very nearly without warning, she was struck down at the height of her renown. Why? What are we to make of it? Why her? It is like some Old Testament parable; these questions were raised five thousand years ago, and we still raise them today. It is the kind of story that stays news, and that is why it must be given prominence. Or so some people believe.

What about the kind of news that doesn't stay news, that is neither the stuff of history nor literature: the fires, rapes, and murders that are daily featured on local television news?

Who has decided that they are important, and why? One cynical answer is that they are there because viewers take comfort in the realization that they have escaped disaster. At least for that day. It doesn't matter who in particular was murdered—the viewer wasn't. We tune in to find out how lucky we are and go to sleep with the pleasure of knowing that we have survived. A somewhat different answer goes this way: it is the task of the news show to provide a daily accounting of the progress of society. This can be done in many ways, some of them abstract (for example, a report on the state of unemployment), some of them concrete (for example, reports on particularly gruesome murders). These reports, especially those of a concrete nature, are the daily facts from which the audience is expected to draw appropriate conclusions about the question "What kind of society am I a member of?" Studies conducted by Professor George Gerbner and his associates at the University of Pennsylvania have shown that people who are heavy television viewers, including viewers of television news shows, believe their communities are much more dangerous than do light television viewers. Television news, in other words, tends to frighten people. The question is, ought they to be frightened? which begs the question, Is the news an accurate portrayal of where we are as a society? Which leads to another question: Is it possible for daily news to give such a picture? Many journalists believe it is possible. Some are skeptical. The early-twentieth-century journalist Lincoln Steffens proved that he could create a "crime wave" anytime he wanted by simply writing about all the crimes that normally occur in a large city during the course of a month. He could also end the "crime wave" by not writing about them. In his autobiography, Steffens describes how he and fellow reporter Jacob Riis started to report New York City street crimes more fully, and sensationally, in their papers. Other reporters followed suit, and suddenly New York's papers were chock full of crime stories and articles about the "crime wave." The same number of muggings, robberies, burglaries, and scams had been going on for years. In fact, there actually had been a recent *reduction* in the number of many crimes!

If crime waves can be manufactured by journalists, how accurate are news shows in depicting the condition of a society? Besides, murders, rapes, and fires (even unemployment figures) are not the only way to assess the progress (or regress) of a society. Why are there so few television stories about symphonies that have been composed, novels written, scientific problems solved, and a thousand other creative acts that occur during the course of a month? Were television news to be filled with these events, we would not be frightened. We would, in fact, be inspired, optimistic, cheerful.

One answer is as follows: these events make poor television news because there is so little to show about them. In the judgment of most editors, people *watch* television. And what they are interested in watching are exciting, intriguing, or exotic pictures. Suppose a scientist has developed a new theory about how to measure with more exactitude the speed with which heavenly objects are moving away from the earth. It is difficult to televise a theory, especially if it involves complex mathematics. You can show the scientist talking about his theory, but that does not make for good television, and too much of it would drive viewers to other stations. In any case, the news show could only give the scientist twenty seconds of airtime because time is an important commodity. Newspapers and magazines sell space, which is not without its limitations for a commercial enterprise. But space can be expanded. Television sells time, and time cannot be expanded. This means that whatever else is neglected, commercials cannot be. Which leads to another possible answer to the question What is news? News, we might say, may be history in its first and best form, or the stuff of literature, or a record of the condition of a society, or the expression of the passions of a public, or the prejudices of journalists. It may be all of those things, but in its worst form it can also be mainly a filler, a come-on, to keep the viewer's attention until the commercials come. Certain producers have learned that by pandering to the audience, by eschewing solid news and replacing it with leering sensationalism, they can essentially present a "television commercial show" interrupted by so-called news.

On February 8, 2007, former Playmate Anna Nicole Smith suddenly died. The Project for Excellence in Journalism reported that her death drew more coverage on cable news than the Iraq war. For that week, her death consumed 21 percent of cable airtime, more than any other story. The Smith story consumed a mind-boggling 50 percent of the cable news hole on February 8 and 9. The day after her death, the research Web site thinkprogress.org reported CNN referred to Anna Nicole Smith 522 percent more frequently than it did to Iraq; and MSNBC, 708 percent. During its coverage, Wolf Blitzer's *The Situation Room* had an average audience of 1.7 million viewers, nearly triple that from the same hour the day before.

In the week ending February 11, ratings for syndicated entertainment news shows were through the roof. *Entertainment Tonight* recorded its best numbers in more than three years. Other programs followed suit: *Inside Edition* was up 11 percent to a new season high; *The Insider* was up 7 percent, a tie for the show's all-time high; and *Extra* was up 4 percent, also to a new season high.

In similar fashion, CNN *Headline News* became America's top-rated cable news network for a full hour in 2006 by showing a car chase in Houston, Texas. No O. J. Simpson, no fugitive from justice, just a car chase. More than 1.5 million viewers watched police chase a car. In another attempt to get more people to watch, the *CBS Evening News* asked its audience to vote on three different stories every Friday. Reporter Steve Hartman would cover the winning story.

One week they voted to send Hartman to Mount Airy, North Carolina, to do a story about a statue of the late actor Don Knotts as his character Barney Fife from *The Andy Griffith Show* (the town already had a statue of Sheriff Andy Taylor and his son, Opie). Need we tell you that *The Andy Griffith Show* aired on CBS? News shows on Fox affiliates seem to think stories about their popular shows *American Idol* and 24 are newsworthy, and the *Today* show welcomes a parade of featured players from NBC programs. In short, news programs have become another venue for promoting the entertainment interests of networks and local stations.

All of which leads us to reiterate, first, that there are no simple answers to the question "What is news?" and, second, that it is not our purpose to tell you what you ought to believe about the question. The purpose of this chapter is to arouse your interest in thinking *about* the question. Your answers are to be found by knowing what you feel is significant and how your sense of the significant conforms with or departs from that of others, including broadcasters, their bosses, and their audiences. Your answers are to be found in your ideas about the purposes of public communication and in your judgment of the kind of society you live in and wish to live in. We cannot provide answers to these questions. But you also need to know something about the problems, limitations, traditions, motivations, and, yes, even the delusions of the television news industry. That's where we can help you to know how to watch television news.

CHAPTER 3

Getting Them into the Electronic Tent

AT CARNIVAL SIDESHOWS, THE barkers used to shout intriguing things to attract an audience. "Step right up. For one thin dime, see what men have died for and others lusted after. The dance of the veils as only Tanya can do it." The crowd would gather as lovely Tanya, wrapped in diaphanous garb, would wiggle a bit, tease and entice grown men who should have known better to part with their money for a ticket. Instead of seeing Tanya shed her clothes, her customers only shed their money.

In television news there is no Tanya that we know of, but there are plenty of Sonyas, Marias, Ricks, and Brads who have the job of getting you into the electronic tent. They come on the air and try to intrigue you with come-ons to get you to watch their show. "Step right up" becomes "coming up at eleven o'clock." And instead of veils you get a glimpse of videotape that may intrigue you enough to part with your time instead of a dime. It is no accident that in the television news industry the short blurb aimed at getting you to watch a program is called a "tease." Sometimes it delivers what it advertises, but often it draws us into the electronic tent and keeps us there long enough that we don't remember why we were there in the first place.

The tease is designed to be very effective, very quickly. By definition, a tease lasts about ten seconds or less, and the information it contains works like a headline. Its purpose is to grab your attention and keep you watching. In the blink of a tease, you are enticed to stay tuned with promises of exclusive stories and tape, good-looking anchors, helicopters, team coverage, hidden cameras, uniform blazers, and even, yes, better journalism. It is all designed to stop you from using the remote-control button to switch channels. But the teasing doesn't stop there. During the news program, just before each commercial, you will see what are known as "bumpers," teases that are aimed at keeping you in the tent and from straying to another channel where other wonders are being touted. And the electronic temptations do not even cease with the end of the program. When the news show is over, you are still being pleaded with "not to turn that dial" and to tune in the next day for an early morning newscast, which in turn will entice you to watch the next news program and so on. If news programmers had it their way, you would watch a steady diet of news programs, one hooking you into the next with only slight moments of relief during station breaks.

If you think you can beat the system by not watching teases, you'll need to think again. We are dealing with serious professional hucksters. On his Web site, Graeme Newell touts himself as a speaker and trainer who shows cable and broadcast teams how to "effectively market and tease their shows." He says he trains broadcast teams how to identify the most sellable components of a show, then teaches specific writing and producing techniques to showcase those strong components. He holds workshops on teasing, and his Web site trumpets, "In most shops, producers are bringing their journalism skills to teasing. But teasing isn't journalism. *Teasing is advertising*" (the emphasis is ours). The game plan, aimed at getting you to watch the news, starts even before you have seen the first tease. It starts while you're watching the entertainment shows before the news. One device used is called the "snipe," an animated graphic that runs at the bottom of the screen, promoting the next show. At the Emmy Awards show in 2007, comedian Lewis Black showed his frustration at snipes, telling the audience, "We don't care about the next show. We're watching this show."

Whether you know it or not, we are programmed to watch the news, by programmers. They know that most of us tend to be lazy. Even with remote controls at our fingertips, we are likely to stay tuned to the channel we have been watching. So the United Couch Potatoes of America sit, and sit, and sit, and before they know it, Marsha and Rick have hooked us into their news program, promising "team coverage," no less, of today's latest disaster. In textbook vernacular, the lead-in programs must leave a residual audience for the news shows that follow. To put it plainly, a station with a strong lineup of entertainment programs can attract a large audience to the news tent. High-rated shows such as *Oprah*, programmed just before the news, bring in a big audience and premium prices at the broadcast marketplace. This is why the best news program may not have ratings as high as a news program with a strong lead-in. It may not be fair, but it is television.

Now, let us say all things are equal. Station A and station B both have excellent lead-ins. What news program will you watch? Most people will say something like, "I want to watch the latest news, the best reporting, with state-of-the-art technology, presented by people I can trust and respect."

But while people might say they like the most experienced journalists presenting the news, many news consultants claim that no matter what they say, the audience prefers to watch good-looking, likable people it can relate to (perhaps of the same age group, race, etc.). News organizations spend a lot of time and money building up the reputations of their anchors, sending them to high-visibility stories they hope will convince viewers they are watching top-level journalists. Unfortunately, in some markets the top anchors are sometimes "hat racks" who read beautifully but can barely type a sentence or two without the aid of a producer and writer. They may know how to anchor, but many are strictly lightweights. In television, looking the part is better than being the real item, a situation you would rightly reject in other contexts. Imagine going to a doctor who hadn't studied medicine but rather looks like a doctor: authoritative, kindly, understanding, and surrounded by formidable machinery. We assume you would reject such a professional fraud, especially if he or she had majored in theater arts in college. But this kind of playacting is perfectly acceptable in the world of television news and entertainment, where actors who have played lawyers on a TV series frequently are called on to give speeches at lawyers' conventions and men who have played doctors are invited to speak at gatherings of medical professionals. If you can read news convincingly on television, you can have a successful career as an anchor, no journalism experience required. This is not to say that there aren't bright men and women who are knowledgeable journalists and who can and do serve as anchors. But the problem is that it is almost impossible for the viewer to figure out which anchor knows his stuff and who's faking it. A good anchor is a good actor, and with the lift of an eyebrow or with studied seriousness of visage, he or she can convince you that you are seeing the real thing; that is, a concerned, solid journalist.

Case in point: actress, bikini model, and former WWE wrestler Lauren Jones signed a thirty-day contract to anchor the news on CBS19 in East Texas starting in June 2007. CBS19 president and general manager Phil Hurley was quoted as saying, "Don't let the blonde hair and modeling credentials fool you . . . she can do the job." However, Ms. Jones had no journalism training or experience; she got the job as a contestant on the Fox show *Anchorwoman*, a program that was canceled after one showing due to awful ratings.

At this point, you may wonder what difference it makes. Even if one cannot distinguish an experienced journalist from a good actor playing the part of an experienced journalist, isn't the news the same? Not quite. An experienced journalist is likely to have a sense of what is particularly relevant about a story, and thus insist on including certain facts, and a perspective the actor-anchor would have no knowledge of. Of course, it is true that often an experienced journalist, working behind the cameras, has prepared the script for the actor-anchor. But when the anchor is himself or herself a journalist, the story is likely to be given additional dimensions. We got a glimpse of this on March 30, 1981, during *ABC Evening News* anchor Frank Reynolds's live news coverage of the assassination attempt on U.S. president Ronald Reagan. All three networks had erroneously reported that White House press secretary James Brady, a close friend of Reynolds's, had died from the head wound he suffered in the incident. After learning on-screen that this information was incorrect, Reynolds suddenly appeared noticeably upset and angrily burst out: "Let's get it *nailed down* . . . somebody . . . let's find out! Let's get it straight so we can report this thing accurately!" The network quickly moved to a break and upon return straightened out the facts.

Even if there are no differences between the stories presented by actor-anchors and journalist-anchors, the fact that the audience is being deluded into thinking that an actor-anchor is a journalist contributes a note of fakery to the enterprise. It encourages producers and news directors to think about what they are doing as artifice, as a show in which truth-telling is less important than the appearance of truth-telling. One can hardly blame them. They know that everything depends on winning the audience's favor, and the anchor is the key weapon in their arsenal.

If you are skeptical about the importance of the anchor in attracting the audience to the electronic tent, you must ask yourself why they are paid so much. It's estimated that Katie Couric signed a contract with CBS worth $15 million a year: $60,000 a day. ABC News' Charles Gibson earned $7 million a year when he took the job in May 2006. Diane Sawyer earns a reported $12 million a year. Brian Williams started out as an NBC anchor at $4 million a year. When the ratings for the *CBS Evening News with Katie Couric* dipped to 5.9 million for a week in 2007, CBS was paying $2.51 per viewer. By comparison, Mr. Gibson was delivering the audience for $0.89 per viewer, and Mr. Williams was a bargain at about $0.55 a head. Even local anchors can be paid as much as $750,000 to $1 million, and that's without serious journalistic credentials. Anchors who work for network-affiliated stations in the top twenty-five markets make an average of $260,000 a year. Nationwide, the average anchor, as of this writing, makes $72,400 a year, according to a Ball State University and Radio-Television News Directors Association (RTNDA) survey.

So there you are, ready to watch the news presented by a high-priced anchor, and on comes the show, complete with a fancy opening and music that sounds as though it was composed for a Hollywood epic. The host appears: an anchor god or goddess sculpted on Mount Arbitron—at least the best of them. But even the worst looks authoritative. Of course, the anchor has had plenty of help from plenty of craftspeople in creating the illusion of calm omniscience. After all, it's not all hair spray. That glittering, well-coiffed, commanding presence has been placed in a setting that has been designed, built, and painted to make him or her look as wonderful as possible. Consultants have been used to make sure the lights are fine-tuned to highlight hair and fill in wrinkles. Color experts have complemented the star's complexion with favorable background hues. Short anchors sit on raised seats to look taller. Makeup has been applied to create just the right look: accenting cheekbones, covering baldness, enlarging small eyes, hiding blemishes, perhaps obscuring a double chin.

And, of course, there is camera magic. A low camera angle can make a slight anchor look imposing. Long and medium shots, rather than close-ups, can hide bags under the eyes. There are lenses that blur facial wrinkles, if necessary. The anchor-star has probably had the benefit of a clothing allowance and the best hairdressers and consultants. At the local level, expert stagecraft is employed. At the pinnacle of TV anchordom, the networks, the best in the craft work their magic.

When Katie Couric took over the *CBS Evening News*, the newscast underwent a massive makeover, from soup to nuts or, in this case, from set to notes. The National Ministry of Design (its actual name, not affiliated with the government) was brought in to create a new look to sweep away the remnants of Dan Rather and "Couricize" the program. The *Boston Globe* reported that designer Jean McCarville said, "the firm began by asking CBS executives to reel off adjectives, ideas about the message they wanted to project. The network offered 'classy,' 'elegant,' and 'timeless.' " CBS wanted to suggest that Couric would be accessible and warm, and have more interaction with reporters and viewers. Ned Biddle, National Ministry's executive producer for the project, recalled executives saying, half-jokingly, that they wanted things to look expensive. So the designers studied ads for expensive things: architecture, cars, jewelry. They noticed a common theme, McCarville says, "a certain shininess" as light glints off diamonds and chrome. They made light virtually glint off the CBS eye logo's letters and curves. To represent Couric, they added warm gold and orange tones. Designers also lifted the curves from the CBS eye and began to wrap nearly everything in them, from the teaser videos at the top of the show to the images that appear over Couric's shoulder as she introduces a story. Woman anchor . . . curves.

The old theme music also had to go. James Horner, the Academy Award–winning composer who has written songs and scores for one hundred movies, including *Titanic*, was called in to write new music: ten seconds of auditory imagery. He met with Couric, and it's reported that *she* told him she wanted something that reminded her of wheat fields instead of the Manhattan skyline. The program's executive producer at the time, Rome Hartman, said he wanted something "flexible, yet memorable. Regal and encompassing the grand history of CBS News, yet moving forward." Joel Beckerman of Man Made Music was also brought in. He supplied more than one hundred short pieces of music, including a dozen variations on the theme, to be used as the mood of the lead story changes from night to night. It is cosmetic television at its finest.

The music fades, and the parade of stories and the people reporting them begins. On the local level, whom you see on the tube depends sometimes on professional competence and journalistic ability. But it may also depend on the results of focus groups where ordinary viewers are shown videotapes and then asked which anchors and reporters they prefer to watch and why. The group gives its opinion without the benefit of observing a performer over a period of time or knowledge of the reporter's background and experience. What is wanted is an immediate, largely emotional reaction. Performers are also evaluated by a service called TVQ, which claims to rate television performers on the basis of public recognition. The company that provides this service, Marketing Evaluations/TVQ, polls about 1,200 Americans by mail. The Q Score is a product of popularity, rated on a scale of one to five, and familiarity among respondents. The results are sold to networks, advertising agencies, and anyone else willing to spend a few thousand dollars to find out someone's Q Score. From time to time, Gallup also does a poll to try to determine the likability of TV personalities. In one poll, Diane Sawyer had the highest overall favorable rating of those tested, followed by Charles Gibson, Matt Lauer, Dan Rather, Regis Philbin, Bob Schieffer, and Brian Williams. Ranking close to the middle were Barbara Walters, Katie Couric, Anderson Cooper, Meredith Vieira, Lou Dobbs, and Larry King. Geraldo Rivera, Star Jones, and Rosie O'Donnell had negative ratings.

Some news-show consultants believe in forming a television news pseudofamily to attract audiences. After the *Today* show started to slide in the ratings in 1991, NBC brought back sportscaster Joe Garagiola to try to pep up ratings. Garagiola had been on the program from 1967 to 1973. NBC had alienated its viewers by replacing popular coanchor Jane Pauley with Deborah Norville, who was supposed to be a hot ratings getter. She wasn't. The show nose-dived. Executives realized they needed something or somebody with pizzazz. They reached for a person who, they hoped, could make the *Today* show a family again: warm, affable Joe Garagiola. The return of the prodigal son. Exit Norville, cast out as the "other woman." The *Today* family is now led by Matt Lauer and Meredith Vieira (who replaced Couric as glamorous mom); Al Roker is the clown weatherman, and Ann Curry does the news. Former clown-weatherman Willard Scott now makes guest appearances with his popular centenarian birthday segments on Tuesdays and Thursdays.

The family concept is at work at many local stations. The anchors will probably be a couple, male and female, both good-looking and in the same relative age category: the husband and wife (although in our modern society, with second marriages common, the male anchor may be twenty years older than his female counterpart). The other "family" members may include an Archie and a Veronica to appeal to the younger set: Archie the sportscaster, who never tires of watching videotapes of highlights and bloopers, and Veronica the weatherperson. There is also Mr. or Ms. Breathless Showbiz who always feigns being thrilled to see the heartthrob or hottest rock group of the moment.

Whatever kind of television family is presented, it always has one thing in common. It is a happy family where everybody gets along with everyone else (at least for thirty minutes) and knows his or her place. The viewer usually gets to see the whole "family" at the top, or beginning, of the show. They will either be featured in a taped introduction or be sitting on the set en masse, to create a sense of cohesion and stability. Throughout the program, members of the family will come to the set and do their turn, depending on their specialty. No newscast is complete without Archie the sportscaster rattling off a list of clichés that he believes bond him to his fans: "Yes!" "In your face!" "Let's go to the videotape!" "Swish!"

Theoretically, sportscasters are supposed to be reporters, not fans. But depending on what they believe to be at the root of their popularity, or what team is featured on their station, they might decide to bask in the glorious light of sports heroes and become cheerleaders. It is, in any event, the sportscaster's job to keep the audience excited with taped highlights and interviews with the top players, who often have nothing more to contribute than standard-brand sports-hero remarks: "It's not important how I played, as long as I can contribute to the team," or "I might have scored a few more touchdowns, but the real credit has to go to the front line who made it all possible." Picture and cliché blend to fill the eye with a sense of action and the nose with the macho smell of the locker room.

No newscast would be complete without a weather report, which usually starts with a review of what already happened that day. The report is supposedly made interesting by moving *H*s and *L*s, and by making clouds and isobars stalk across a map. Whatever the weather, the one thing you can always count on is a commercial break *before* tomorrow's weather forecast. You can also count on the peculiar tendency of anchors to endow the weatherperson with godlike meteorological powers: "Well, Veronica, I hope you'll bring us some relief from this rain." To which the reply is something like, "Oh, Chuck, I'm afraid we've got some more rain coming tomorrow, but wait till you see what I've got for you this weekend."

If you have ever wondered why all this fuss is made about the weather, the answer is that, for reasons no one knows, weather information is of almost universal interest. This means that it usually attracts an attentive audience, which in turn means it provides a good environment for commercials. An executive producer of the *CBS This Morning* show has remarked that research shows weather news is the most important reason why people watch TV in the morning. The weather segments also give the anchors a chance to banter with the weather people and lighten the proceedings. A pleasing personality is almost certainly more important to a weathercaster than a degree in meteorology. How significant personality is can be gauged by what these weather people earn. Weather people in small markets earn an average of $21,980 a year, according to the National Association of Broadcasters. Weathercasters make an average of $91,000 in the top twenty-five markets, with some earning a $500,000 or more. Nonetheless, it should not surprise you to know that weathercasters rarely prepare weather forecasts. There are staff meteorologists for that. The on-air weatherperson is expected to draw audiences, not weather maps.

Feature reporters usually ply their craft near the "back of the book," close by the weather. They keep the mood light and try to leave the viewer with a smile. The subject matter of some feature vignettes is called "evergreen" because it is not supposed to wilt with the passage of time. It can be stored until needed. (Two of the best practitioners of "evergreen art" were Charles Kuralt and Andy Rooney.) Locally, you usually see evergreen reports on slow news days, when the editor has trouble filling the news budget (the newsworthy events of the day). But as entertaining news becomes more of a commodity, feature reports are being used more and more to attract and hold audiences through the news program.

No news family would be complete without a science reporter, a Dr. Wizard, who usually wears glasses, may have an advanced degree, and is certainly gray around the temples. These experts bring to the audience the latest in everything from cancer research to the designer disease of the year. Some with the title "Dr." may actually be MDs, but don't count on it.

Once the family has gathered, everyone in place and with a specific role, the show is ready to begin. The anchor reads the lead story. If you are expecting to hear the most important news on any given day, you will often be disappointed. Never forget that the program's producer is trying to grab you before you zap away to another news show. Therefore, chances are you will hear a tease about a story such as Paris Hilton's visit to jail, Pamela Anderson's home videos, happenings in the British royal family, or news of a Beyoncé tour. Those stories have glitter and glamour in today's journalism. And if glitter and glamour won't do the job, gore will. Body bags have become an important currency in TV news, and a four-bagger is a grand slam.

An all-important attraction to a news show is called a "get"; that is, when a newsperson can line up a headliner who will attract an audience. For example, the *New York Times*'s Jim Rutenberg reported in 2003, when rescued POW Jessica Lynch was going to give her first interview after returning from Iraq, that CBS News offered her a two-hour documentary with CBS News, a TV movie with CBS Entertainment, the chance to cohost a special on MTV, and a book deal with Simon & Schuster. Need we tell you that CBS, MTV, and Simon & Schuster are all owned by Viacom? Diane Sawyer got this "get" and interviewed Jessica Lynch first on TV. When famous croc hunter Steve Irwin died in 2006, published reports said ABC News coughed up $1 million or more for an interview with his widow by Barbara Walters and a "licensing fee" for footage of the daredevil who was killed by a stingray. ABC News insisted it did not pay for the interview, but a source at NBC News said it dropped out of the bidding when the price became "insane." Reports say that NBC once offered singer Michael Jackson $5 million for an interview and other footage, with the promise of postponing a tough *Dateline NBC* report on him. That deal fell through. A 2001 inside.com story ranked Monica Lewinsky's first television interview as the biggest get of all time.

If viewers have stayed through the lead story, they probably will be hooked for a while because the newscast is designed to keep their attention through the commercial breaks into the next section, when the process starts again. Taped stories from reporters are peppered throughout the show to keep interest from flagging as anchors keep the program on track, "eyeballing," or reading, stories on camera. When the news stories thin out, there are sports, features, and weather to fill up the time.

All this is presented with slick lighting and production values, moving along at a crisp pace. The tempo is usually fast since some programmers believe that fast-paced news programs attract younger audiences. Older audiences, they believe, are attracted to a slower-paced, quieter presentation. As such, trying to simulate the experience of the banner-ad-plastered Internet, some news shows are cluttering their screens with information. The *New York Times* reports, "on CNN, the hyperactive pace of Wolf Blitzer's nightly news show 'The Situation Room' is so extreme that it was parodied on 'Saturday Night Live.' " With one glance at the screen, is it really possible to absorb the United States military strategy in Iraq or that a thunderstorm is moving over the Midwest, the Standard & Poor's index is up 16.95 points, and Sean Combs has separated from his girlfriend? No matter how cluttered or fast or slow the pace of the show, there is not much time to present anything but truncated information. For his weekly *Tyndall Report*, news analyst Andrew Tyndall analyzed the content of the first night of *CBS Evening News with Katie Couric*. He says the program averaged about 8.1 minutes of hard news and 10.9 minutes of features, interviews, and commentary: about 19 minutes of content. On average, the nightly half-hour network newscasts contain seven taped news packages (as a complete recorded story is known). And that's almost 85 percent of the time spent filling the news hole. According to the annual "State of the News Media" report, at the local level viewers get "a lot of local weather, traffic, and crime. As for other news of the day—local or national—usually just three or four items received anything more than a brief anchor report with taped sound." And, of course, more time must be subtracted if there's "happy talk" on the set. Tyndall figures that morning shows average 42.5 minutes of news each hour.

Given the limited time and objectives of a television newscast, the viewer has to realize that he or she is not getting a full meal but rather a snack. And depending on the organization presenting the news, that snack may contain plenty of empty calories.

CHAPTER 4

Donuts, Big Foot, Mules, and the Bird

UP TO THIS POINT, we have taken what some might regard as a cynical perspective on TV news. We think we have been more realistic than cynical. And we wish to continue to be realistic. Which means that although the competitive news wars are fought by anchor-personalities, there are others who are indispensable to the victories. As in real wars, the spectacular heroes always get the headlines, but it is the foot soldiers who win the battles by grinding out the victories day by day, inch by inch. In the TV wars, the foot soldiers are the general-assignment reporters who crank out stories whether the amount of news is a flood or a trickle. In the trade, they are known as "mules" because they work long hours, travel far, and carry the burden of getting and presenting stories of significant substance, even if such stories are neither glamorous nor intriguing. As the networks' audience shrinks, they have repeatedly cut such staff. At Arizona State University, Dr. Joe Foote found that the number of reporters who appear on network news has declined from a peak of 76.7 in 1985 to 50 in 2002, which is a drop of 35 percent.

The reduction in reporting staff means an increase in workload. In 1985, reporters did an average 31.4 stories a year on the evening newscast. By 2002, according to Foote, that number had climbed to 40.9. Sometimes the reporter will "front" stories, that is, do stories developed by other staff people. We gain insight into the process through Dan Rather's $70 million lawsuit against CBS in September 2007, in which he describes the reasons he was fired. In the court papers, Rather indicates he was little more than a narrator of the disputed broadcast that purported to offer new evidence of preferential treatment given to President George W. Bush when he was a lieutenant in the Air National Guard. Instead of directly vetting the script he would read on air for that segment, Rather said he acceded to pressure from the CBS news chief and focused instead on reporting his other stories. He said he "played largely a supervisory role." It should be noted that the former executive producer of *60 Minutes II*, Josh Howard, who was forced to resign over the story, refuted the charge, saying Rather "did every interview. He worked the sources over the phone. He was there in the room with the so-called document experts. He argued over every line in the script. It's laughable."

If the mule works well out in the field, he or she may be promoted to the status of a "big foot." A big foot is a reporter who is sent to the major stories that are sure to attract attention and may become the lead stories on any particular show. The big feet are star reporters and often earn big dollars, although never as much as a star anchor. Big feet may even have their own staffs, including a field producer. Dr. Foote (whose name only coincidentally calls to mind his scholarly interest) has kept an eye on big feet and has concluded that any network correspondent picked to cover the "iron triangle" of the White House, the Pentagon, and the State Department, or anyone involved in coverage of a presidential election, has career success guaranteed.

At contract-negotiation time, a big foot may demand prominent display on the air, special perks including clothing allowances, jobs for assistants, and, in one case we know of, even her own hairdresser. In return, he or she is expected to pick up at a moment's notice and travel just about anywhere news is breaking. And they are absolutely expected to get their story on the air that night. The best among them can earn between $100,000 and $275,000 a year in the large markets, even at a local level. In smaller cities, of course, they may make much less. According to a 2007 RTNDA / Ball State University Survey, a news reporter working for the average television station in the United States makes about $35,600 a year. In the smallest markets, the median pay is $20,000 for reporters. In the top twenty-five markets, including New York, Los Angeles, and Chicago, they earn median pay of $56,000 a year. Network reporting stars may earn between $100,000 and a few million dollars if they are prominently featured on a show.

But don't dash out to buy a trench coat and hair spray for your new career as a correspondent until you hear about some of the drawbacks. For openers, it can be very dangerous. The International Federation of Journalists reports that the year 2006 was the deadliest for journalists and news media workers worldwide, with 177 journalists and media staff killed. Most of them were victims of premeditated attack or caught in the crossfire of war, but 22 died in accidents or natural disasters.

Iraq was the most dangerous place to work, and 103 journalists and 39 media support workers have been killed there while doing their jobs since March 2003. Forty-eight journalists have been abducted since the start of the U.S.-led invasion. CBS News correspondent Kimberly Dozier was seriously wounded by a roadside bomb that killed a CBS cameraman and soundman in Iraq. ABC anchor Bob Woodruff and his cameraman were seriously injured by a roadside explosion while traveling with Iraqi troops.

In comparison to the danger, reporter's complaints of long hours may seem trivial, but the job can be exhausting. You might see a reporter doing a stand-up on the screen for just a few seconds, but it may have taken ten hours to get the story and the pictures to match. Think about it. On radio, a reporter could say, "The camels came over the Alps carrying food and guns, as a fierce storm lashed the animals and their masters with hard hailstones." It might take a few minutes to write that script or a few moments to ad-lib it, but to put that same scene on television is a camel with a different hump. Imagine how difficult it would be to videotape the pictures to match that description. And if the event happened at night on a steep bit of terrain, it would be even more difficult to record. Television reporters may have to drive miles or wait on a stakeout for hours just to get a simple shot that will last five or ten seconds on the screen. It's hard work. Many reporters get to work at eight in the morning. They may be sent to the courthouse, a fire, or a crane collapse, depending on what is happening that day. Let's say a reporter is assigned coverage of an important trial. If she is in the right position at the entrance the defendants use, she may get pictures and manage to shout a quick question before the court convenes. Leaving the camera crew in position, the reporter dashes to the courtroom to cover the case and tries to absorb the more esoteric points of law. She may talk with attorneys and other observers during the breaks to gain further insights. At the end of the daily court session, the reporter must decide what tape, if any, to use; she may want to shoot the work of courtroom artists; she'll have to line up on-camera interviews, write a comprehensive and easily understandable script, learn it, and be prepared to go on the air live, while giving the impression that she is in total control of the situation. Having done that for the early news, the reporter may be asked by the producer to provide a live presence at the courthouse for the late news. The reporter may watch the fifteenth hour slip by before being able to get home, fall into bed, and dream of torts and rules of evidence before starting over again the next day. With all-news cable outlets like Court TV and CNN, reporters may be on call at any hour, 24–7, appearing on the drive-time morning and afternoon news, with appearances on nightly news talk shows.

Not too long ago, the reporter had to wait for film to be developed before a visual story could be presented on the air. Now, digital video provides instant pictures, which solves the problem of processing delays. But the newfound speed has caused other problems. For example, the audience expects to see events on the tube quickly, if not live. With the advent of satellite technology, a reporter may fly to the scene of a story, dig to get the information and pictures she needs, then file a series of individually tailored reports for several stations, each with specific needs. If the stations are in different time zones, the work can be grueling, albeit with high visibility and pay.

Years ago, if there was major news, the public might see pictures of the event in their movie theaters a week or so later. But since we now expect to see live pictures from the scene almost immediately on TV, a new dimension has been added to the news-show wars. News departments compete with one another to be first in delivering the pictures. Each network usually budgets between $200,000 and $300,000 a month for special-event coverage: $3 million or $4 million a year. But when many major international stories happen, all stops are pulled out. Events such as the invasion of Iraq or Lebanon can cost a network millions of dollars to cover. Television stations are fierce in their desire to be first to get a picture from the scene on the air. On the plus side, we get to see the view from the camera's eye, quickly and relatively unfettered. But there is a price we pay for supersonic journalism: the historic function of journalism is either forgotten or distorted. In the frantic quest to be first with footage or even a "fast-breaking" story that is unaccompanied by pictures, TV news departments do not have the time, resources, or the interest to explain the meaning of the event. Journalism is supposed to present facts in an accurate and orderly fashion. It is also supposed to place the facts in some political or sociological context so that viewers have some sense of how to weigh the facts and what value to give to them.

About the only concession news departments make to this tradition is to call upon "political experts," usually a nervous-looking person from Georgetown University. The anchor asks the expert if this story is important and what will happen from here. The expert answers that the story is very important and only time will tell about the future. This charade takes about thirty seconds.

The real "experts" turn out to be the reporters racing to the scene of stories, often arriving just minutes before airtime. What kinds of experts are they? Well, often they are filled in on story details from their assignment editors via mobile radios or cellular phones while they're en route to the scene. What this means is that TV reporters dash to the microphone with just a smattering of knowledge and bounce the slim reportage off a satellite to your home. While the image of an event hurtles through the air with enormous speed, the perspective that comes with thoughtful reflection is thrown to the wind in favor of "now you see it, now you don't" journalism. Of course, there are some experienced, talented reporters who can grasp stories quickly and report effectively on the run. And they will be more and more in demand for their ability to ad-lib and process information quickly as new technologies are developed to deliver the news even faster. But the average reporter is not able to keep up with warp speed, and most of the time we will have to settle for reporting that has little substance, if any.

The competitive drive to get the story on the air quickly, and the technological ability to do so, obviously reduces the ability of journalists to check facts and other information. When the news is transmitted instantaneously, without the benefit of a gatekeeper or journalist to review it before airing, the results can be dramatic but at times false and misleading. A special report for CNN shows

> the results of the United States presidential election of 2000, conducted on November 7, were not finally known until 36 days later, making this election one of the most drawn-out, confusing, acrimonious and controversial elections in the nation's history. The confusion and controversy began on Election Night itself, when the television networks committed serious errors in their reporting of the election returns. Most serious were: The report that Vice President Al Gore, the Democratic candidate, had won the key state of Florida, followed later by a retraction of that report. . . . The erroneous Gore calls were made by ABC, CBS, CNN, Fox News, and NBC, as well as by the Associated Press.

There were also misinformed reports "that Texas governor George W. Bush, the Republican candidate, had won Florida, and with it the presidency." This led to Gore's concession to Bush by telephone, based on the erroneous information, and yet another retraction by the networks—this time for announcing Bush as the winner. The later announcements of Bush's winning were made by the five television networks but not by the Associated Press.

Another unvetted story reported by CBS and ABC news helped convince the American public that the United States should attack Iraqi forces occupying Kuwait. In 1990, before the United States went to war, a congressional caucus heard testimony, supposedly from a Kuwaiti refugee, telling of inhuman horror. The witness, Nayirah al-Sabah, told of watching Iraqi troops as they took babies out of incubators in a Kuwaiti hospital, put them on a cold floor to die, and removed the incubators, apparently for shipment to Iraq. The television picture was dramatic. The witness cried as she told her story, and the moving testimony, later quoted by President Bush in speeches, may have helped convince the American public and Congress to go to war against Iraq. But it has since been revealed that the "eyewitness" was in reality the daughter of the Kuwaiti ambassador to the United States. It was further alleged that she had been coached by the public relations firm Hill and Knowlton, whose client, Citizens for a Free Kuwait, was primarily funded by the emir of Kuwait. According to Kuwaiti doctors interviewed by *20/20* and *60 Minutes*, no such incidents of killing babies had occurred.

One way local producers deal with the lightning speed of information transmission is to prepare some segments of live news events in advance. This is accomplished by preparing a "donut." A donut includes a live intro by the reporter, on camera, in the field, followed by a taped, edited segment and then a live "outro." This is why, when you see a report on television, you usually hear the latest news from the reporter live on the scene, who then introduces older taped material and finally brings you up to date live at the end of the report: a "donut."

What we are talking about here, and is a constant obstacle in TV journalism, is the pressure of time. Time works against understanding, coherence, and even meaning. The practical needs of a show, especially getting on the air at a specific time, call for the reporter to do the best he can under the circumstances. The producer may also want a live stand-up at the scene of a story, requiring valuable travel time. Network affiliate stations frequently want live on-scene reports regardless of differences in time zones. News producers, operating from a distance and shielded from the difficulties in the field, can make unnecessary and impractical demands. And the plethora of morning-news and business shows can make certain stories round-the-clock assignments. The correspondent may be whipped in five directions at once and be expected to be well-informed and composed while presenting an in-depth report. All this, and a glamorous demeanor too.

In fact, no matter how much effort, intelligence, and craft a television reporter may bring to a story, viewer mail will invariably bring comments about the reporter's appearance. A reporter can hang out of a helicopter, get great pictures, and tell a cohesive story, but that's not good enough for some viewers, who will complain that the reporter's hair was standing up. Some viewers will request the name of his tailor. That is why some reporters will go to greater lengths to look good than to get the full story. Dan Rather, who had an illustrious career, is still known as Gunga Dan because of the full native dress he donned when he snuck across the border from Pakistan to Afghanistan in 1980. But newspeople not only dress to impress their viewers, they put on airs. Besides the clothing they wear, television journalists often wear titles. In these days of hyperbole, puffery, and imagery, a reporter for even the smallest station may be called a correspondent or, even better, a senior correspondent (whatever that is) simply because the news director gives him the label. Years ago, men and women who pounded the pavements reporting stories were called reporters. A few exalted network icons were promoted to the rank of correspondent by virtue of experience, knowledge, and journalistic ability. No more. Now everyone is at least a correspondent.

Perhaps the glamorous names have something to do with the glamorous technologies that are now so much a part of the news industry. "Reporter" is a word associated with a pad and pencil, a portable typewriter, and an old-fashioned dial telephone. "Correspondent" suggests a new era. New times, some say, require new words. And these are certainly new times. During the past decade, the way a reporter gets the job done has radically changed. The *Washington Journalism Review* gives one dramatic example told by CBS News associate producer David Hawthorne. He was on a flight leaving New York's City's LaGuardia Airport for North Carolina on his way to cover Hurricane Hugo. The plane aborted takeoff and crashed into the water. Hawthorne helped several mothers get their children onto the wing of the plane, then managed to climb back into the shattered fuselage to retrieve his cell phone from under his seat. He immediately called CBS and, from the crash site, was put on the air with Dan Rather for the first live report from the scene. In October 2006, Yankee pitcher Cory Lidle's plane crashed into a New York apartment building. Scott Wilder, a cameraman for Fox News, was on another assignment twenty blocks away when the crash occurred. He raced to the scene and reported live with a handheld Palm Treo Smartphone that used the existing mobile network to transmit streaming video.

Not only professionals are taking advantage of new technology. Citizen journalists are changing the face of TV news. When grad student Jamal Albarghouti heard gunshots on the campus of Virginia Tech on April 16, 2007, he took out his Nokia mobile phone and started taking shaky but compelling video of police scrambling and the sound of twenty-seven gunshots. Thirty-two people were shot to death on the campus before the gunman took his own life. Not only was the deadliest shooting spree in U.S. history recorded by new technology, but students reported text messaging one another with information while hiding under their desks. Later, some students shared their experiences on sites such as Facebook and collegemedia.com, and many student blogs recounted the dramatic story. Amateurs have used their lightweight, inexpensive camcorders and camera phones to broaden news coverage for years. On October 17, 1989, Debra Kelly was driving home to Oklahoma from a West Coast vacation when an earthquake struck northern California. As it happened, Debbie was on the San Francisco Bay Bridge when part of the bridge collapsed. She was able to shoot one of the most famous shots of the catastrophe: a car plunging off the collapsed section of the bridge. George Holliday's videotape of the beating of Rodney King by Los Angeles policemen had enormous impact across the nation. With more people like George Holliday and Jamal Albarghouti recording events as they happen, news directors are predicting widespread use of amateur videos on newscasts in the future.

Camcorders, cell phones, and laptop computers may be helpful, but nothing has been more influential to television news reporting than the satellite, which allows television signals to be bounced from earth to space and back quickly and relatively inexpensively. In November 1989, the Berlin Wall fell when the East German government allowed its citizens to travel to West Berlin. Hundreds of thousands of Germans gathered at the wall. So did hundreds of anchormen and anchorwomen. Local TV viewers watched something that had been crumbling for some time: the illusion that only networks could bring the public news from the far corners of the earth. The launch of communications satellites, known in the TV business as "birds," resulted in local audiences getting a bird's-eye view of the world. The satellites are launched into a pattern 22,300 miles above the earth and move in a geosynchronous orbit so that each satellite remains over the same spot on earth. This allows signals to be sent to the satellites and bounced back to earth for reception almost anywhere on the planet.

Once upon a time, NBC linked both coasts of the United States via coaxial cable, showing the Atlantic and Pacific at the same time on a split screen. It was an expensive technology requiring the laying of a thick cable from coast to coast and to every television station receiving the signal. Now, local stations, which could not afford to send television signals via cables, are able to get a signal from just about anywhere. In the blink of an eye, about a half second, satellite technology makes it possible for a local station to present pictures from multiple locations on-screen simultaneously. Local stations can get their anchors on a plane and put them on the air from the Wailing Wall, the walls of the Kremlin, the Berlin Wall, the Great Wall of China, or any other wall worthy of international notice. Supported by tape from sources including CNN, local news operations can now present their audiences with the same stories as the networks. This was quite evident during the Hurricane Katrina disaster in 2005. The storm was the third-strongest hurricane ever recorded to make landfall in the United States. Television audiences saw meteorological pictures of the storm forming over the Bahamas on August 23, 2005, then watched it hit land in Florida and finally the Louisiana-Mississippi state line, devastating New Orleans on the morning of August 29. Audiences watched the wind and flooding destroy homes and lives. Television showed thousands of people jam the convention center and Superdome, many without food, water, and proper sanitary conditions. Amazingly, Federal Emergency Management Agency director

Michael Brown told ABC's Ted Koppel on September 1, 2005, that "we just learned of the convention center—we being the federal government—today." Koppel responded, "Don't you guys watch television? Don't you guys listen to the radio? Our reporters have been reporting on it for more than just today."

The digital video recorder has turned just about anyone with a camcorder into a photojournalist. Dramatic pictures taken by amateurs recorded the September 11, 2001, suicide attacks on the World Trade Center in New York. Other dramatic videos captured the tsunami that smashed parts of Thailand in 2004 and killed about three hundred thousand people. The aftermath of the London terrorist bombings in 2006, in which fifty-two people were killed, was taped by scores of amateurs. During the Iraq war, the *New York Times* reported that videos showing insurgent attacks against American troops were being shown on popular Internet video-sharing sites, including YouTube and Google Video. Many of the videos, showing sniper attacks against Americans and roadside bombs exploding under American military vehicles, were posted not by insurgents or their official supporters but by Internet users in the United States and other countries, who passed along videos found elsewhere. While they are not news oriented, on YouTube alone sixty-five thousand new videos are uploaded every twenty-four hours. Yahoo! News and other Web sites are trying to mobilize the video cell phones and digital handicams of the world into a new citizen journalist–powered video project, including "You Witness News."

On a professional level, "videojournalists"—reporters who carry cameras, shoot stories, and also report them—are ubiquitous. This form of journalism requires someone with more than good looks and charm. It calls for a person capable of operating a camera while narrating the scene. There are those who predict that the networks will eventually close their worldwide bureaus and rely on stringer (nonstaff reporter) videojournalists. Can a journalist ferret out the facts while operating as a one-man band? Will the artistry of the picture suffer? No one knows yet. But there is no question that advancing technology makes the videojournalist not only a specialist at the network level but an economic necessity.

Economics are pushing major news organizations in other ways as well. For almost fifty years, the three networks dominated international news coverage not only because of their technological and financial resources but also because of their commitment to excellence. During World War II, Edward R. Murrow built the CBS News team, recruiting top-level print newsmen for radio. They helped invent broadcast news at its best, and that tradition was carried over to television. The other networks built news departments of global depth and experience in a similar fashion. Many experienced journalists remained at the same network for most of their careers out of loyalty and commitment. But in the 1980s, with the three networks run by corporate conglomerates, commitment to the dollar replaced commitment to excellence. News bureaus' personnel and budgets were cut back. Veteran reporters who had risked their lives in Vietnam and other danger spots were discharged—all this while a few well-known anchors and reporters demanded and received extravagant salaries. Former CBS News president Fred Friendly called the situation a "harvest of greed," a reference to the famous CBS documentary by Edward R. Murrow, *Harvest of Shame*. Friendly told an "Ethics and Television" seminar that high-priced stars like Dan Rather and Diane Sawyer should voluntarily give up one third of their salaries to save the jobs of hundreds of CBS employees cut in the financial crunch in the late 1980s. Friendly remarked, "No journalist requires one or two or three million dollars a year." It is, he believes, "unhealthy, unacceptable, and unethical" for television journalists to make ten times more than the president of the United States and twenty times more than members of Congress. Friendly made no allies among the superstar news personalities by adding, "For these talented and dedicated journalists to stand idly, while the important foundations of the best and most comprehensive team in broadcasting journalism anywhere begins to crumble, approaches an exercise in unethical behavior."

Friendly's reproaches notwithstanding, reporters and other news talent took note of the new corporate climate, and many sold their services to the highest bidder. In effect, the networks became homogenized as anchors and reporters switched call letters. CBS's Diane Sawyer moved to ABC for a reported $6 million a year (her salary has now doubled to $12 million). Barbara Walters jumped from NBC to ABC to become the first woman to coanchor an evening network news program. Brit Hume and Chris Wallace went to cable. And so on. Dan Rather was shoved out of CBS following the Killian documents controversy, also known as Memogate, in which he broadcast a story involving unauthenticated documents critical of President George W. Bush's National Guard service record.

As defection followed defection, the unique elements that defined each network disappeared. Behind the scenes, news producers and writers also switched allegiances and jobs. Network news shows began looking and sounding alike: leading with similar stories and often featuring reporters and anchors who had formerly worked for the competition. Indeed, following the war in the Persian Gulf, where pool reporting was the norm, the networks decided to try to pool certain coverage at the White House and some trips by the president. Networks are also jumping into pooling arrangements with their Internet sites. In August 2007, CBS News and the *Washington Post* announced they would be teaming up to share content on their respective Web properties during the 2008 presidential campaign. Washingtonpost.com will feature video snippets from CBS News staffers reporting on key campaign developments, while CBSNews.com will publish new analysis and commentary produced by *Washington Post* political reporters. In addition, reporters from both organizations will participate in a series of interactive forums, and both sites' reporting staffs plan to collaborate to produce several larger stories as part of the partnership. NBC News and the *New York Times* announced they are teaming up to cover the 2008 presidential election. As part of the collaboration, NBC News will "have first access to breaking news" reported by the *Times* and vice versa. "This collaboration gives our organizations the ability to cover all the bases, with a powerhouse combination of top-quality journalism and top-flight technology delivering the story to viewers and readers wherever, and whenever, they want it," said Mark Lukasiewicz, vice president of digital media for NBC News.

As early as 1991, CBS News and Ted Turner's Cable News Network had decided to share a news bureau in Berlin. The two networks kept separate editorial staffs, correspondents, and producers, but they decided to use the same office facilities and technical operations, including satellite equipment. They estimated the shared arrangement would save a total of $400,000 a year. Apparently, the savings are greater than the need to function as an independent news source. Nowadays, the mix-and-match network operations often are separated by just fractions of a point in the ratings since they all serve up similar fare.

In local news, the battle lines between rival news operations are being blurred even more. An RTNDA survey shows that a fair number of news directors report providing their news content to another TV station. In 2006, nearly three-dozen markets had deals where one TV station produced a newscast for another. *Broadcasting & Cable*'s Allison Romano reported that producing a newscast for another channel in town can add up to $1 million to a station's revenues. In 2005, 21 percent of news directors reported supplying news to another station. That is slightly lower than the year before (23 percent) but higher than 2003 (18 percent). The RTNDA survey's author, Bob Papper, estimates that more than 150 newsrooms are now producing news for multiple stations, a significant trend in the industry. To give one example, ABC affiliate WNEP-TV produces a newscast in Scranton, Pennsylvania, for the local Fox Broadcasting Company affiliate, WOLF-TV.

This revolution in TV news did not come about in a vacuum. Developments in the public and private sector shattered the traditional TV-news mold. The developments included the relaxed licensing standards of the FCC, the economic squeeze on TV stations and networks, and increased competition from cable and the Internet. In fact, the remarkable formation of CNN, the all-news network, by Ted Turner, changed the way networks operated and perceived their news mission. Before CNN, if you wanted to watch the news on national television you had to wait for the half hour of news from one of the three networks at dinnertime. If you missed it, you missed TV network news. But suddenly CNN news was there, not only for a half hour a day, but whenever you wanted it (providing, of course, that you had cable). CNN has indeed become a public utility like the telephone, electricity, or water. You turn on the faucet and out pours the news. At the beginnings of CNN in 1980, the networks hoped that such an operation would be too costly and technologically complex for a maverick entrepreneur in Atlanta, Georgia, to pull off. In fact, in network newsrooms CNN was sometimes derisively known as the Chicken Noodle News. But CNN not only covered the news in a journalistically solid fashion but gained an excellent reputation for being first with major stories and staying on the air with them longer than the networks. The success of CNN begat all-news MSNBC and the Fox News Channel, among other outlets.

Blocked by FCC regulations against owners of entertainment programs, the networks realized that while they couldn't broadcast news around the clock, they could develop news programs that (1) were relatively cheap to produce, (2) could turn a profit, and (3) could do so without necessarily attracting huge audiences. For example, the CBS show *48 Hours* can be produced for about $400,000 and returns $800,000 to $900,000 in profits per show, even though it often finishes low on the list of the nation's most popular shows (at one time, sixty-fourth out of eighty-three shows in prime time). Moreover, producers have not been squeamish about wrecking the reputation for seriousness and dignity that network news departments once deserved. Conservative NBC has broadcast a Geraldo Rivera special on devil worship, and ABC and CBS have featured dramatic re-creations on their news programs.

The staid and once-serious network news has begun to look like glitzy local news operations. To the charge that the networks are now money machines and nothing more, and that the old days were better, the answer has come back that CBS once featured Edward R. Murrow visiting the homes of celebrities via television and that Walter Cronkite was once paired with a puppet in an attempt to get ratings for a CBS morning program. These are not convincing answers, and it is hard to find network executives or journalists who believe them. The networks have always been largely concerned about making money, but at an earlier time they felt keenly their obligation to operate first-class news departments even if it meant running them at a deficit. That sort of thinking is now as obsolete as coaxial cable.

CHAPTER 5

Behind the Scenes: Nuts and Bolts

THE NUMBER OF PEOPLE required to put together a TV news show is seemingly endless. Their names usually appear about once a week on the crawl at the end of a newscast, perhaps squeezed over to the side of the TV picture. The names fly by from the top to the bottom of the screen as an announcer distracts you by asking you to stay tuned for the next program. Nonetheless, if you could transport yourself onto the stage set at the television station you might be surprised at the small number of people in the studio. At one point, most major newscasts had at least three camera operators shooting the in-studio pictures of the anchors, a floor director, lighting experts, stage-hands, weather people, and other performers on the set. But automation and robotics changed all that. Now some news programs, including network shows, have robot cameras moving around the studio floor to shoot the various angles selected by the director. If you watch the same newscast night after night, you will notice virtually the same studio shots, in the same order, repeated from show to show. There might be a master wide shot of the anchor sitting handsomely on the set as the announcer introduces the program. This is followed by a medium head-on shot of the anchor as he or she reads the introduction to the first story, followed by videotape. The next story may involve a camera change, with the anchor looking left or right, and so on. The camera positions are rehearsed from time to time to present the on-set talent in the best possible light. Since the shots are predictable, the camera moves are sometimes pre-programmed and stored in computers. As each camera is activated, a red light next to the lens is turned on. When human camera operators are present, they can jockey the cameras around as instructed by the director, who is in the control room. The floor manager is in charge of the camera crew on the studio floor. She gets instructions from the control room through a headset utilizing IFB. (IFB stands for "interruptible fold back." The name came about from broadcast applications where the audio from the program being produced was fed back to on-camera talent via an earphone of some type. The program feed was interrupted by the producer to cue the talent for scene changes, etc. as the production was in process.) The floor manager cues the talent by using hand signals. She might alert the anchor to the next "hot camera," counting down the time to the next video or indicating a camera change. The floor manager is the human lifeline between the talent on the set and the control room.

Also out of camera range is the TelePrompTer operator. She is the person who helps the anchor look like he's memorized his script as he focuses with intensive eye contact on the camera. It is her job to keep the script up-to-date, make changes, operate the TelePrompTer, and keep the script scrolling at the reading pace of the anchors. If the TelePrompTer operator scrolls too slowly, the anchors have to slow their reading down; if she scrolls too fast, the anchor could start sounding like Alvin the Chipmunk, trying to keep up the pace. The TelePrompTer operator may use a manual device on which actual pieces of typed script paper are laid out on a moving belt; in more modern facilities, the computerized script appears on a screen. In either event, the script is projected onto a piece of glass located directly over the camera lens. This allows the anchor to look directly into the camera, as if making eye contact with the viewer, while reading the copy. We've all seen situations where anchors suddenly stop talking and stumble a bit, then look down at their scripts. Chances are something went awry with the TelePrompTer, forcing the anchors to rely on hard copy, scripts printed on paper used as backups. One of the skills of the better anchors is to cover up these awkward moments, perhaps by ad-libbing. There have been situations where a TelePrompTer has died just before airtime, requiring the professionalism of the anchors and crew to prevent a "crash and burn" situation.

Unlike in radio, the anchor-reader does not have to be in eye contact with the control room. It is not unusual for control rooms to be located in another area, perhaps a different floor or building. There, the producer, director, assistant director (AD), technical director (switcher), audio operator, still store / Chyron (or a digital system such as Deko, Thunder, or iNFiNiT!) operator, video operator, remote coordinator, lighting director, and other editorial personnel monitor and guide the program on the air.

The producer, of course, is the captain of the ship, responsible for getting the broadcast on the air. He makes the key editorial decisions including when each story is aired, its length, and its position in the program. He works hand in hand with the director, who is in charge of the technical phase of the broadcast including calling all the shots and directing cameras, graphics, and remote pickups. The director's rhythm, pace, and shot selection play an important part in the look and feel of a newscast. The technicians follow the orders of the director, who determines what picture goes on the air. When the director calls for a story, it will be played back in one of two ways. With the older analog technology, the engineer in a separate room pushes a button that "rolls" the cassette tape. Each tape has a "countdown" on it—ten, nine, eight, and so on—and, with correct timing, the first video picture should come on the air on cue. When that tape has been played, the engineer cues up the next tape in a playback machine and again waits for orders from the director. The more modern technology utilizes digital playback. The stories are stored in servers and "fire," or playback, instantly at the push of a button or touch on a screen.

The assistant director helps the director by cuing, counting down taped segments where necessary, and keeping track of the timing of individual stories and the newscast as a whole. She will advise the producer and director if the show is on time or in need of more material. Based on her calculations, material may be cut or added to have the show "time out."

The technical director is the link between the control room and what goes out over the air. The technical director operates a switcher, which looks like a control board with a panel of buttons, slides, and switches. The equipment is connected to all the possible sources of news, including digital servers or tape machines, live remotes, and the studio. Commercials are played from "master control." Using such devices as Quantels, the switcher has a bag of electronic tricks at her fingertips. She can make a picture appear in a little box, or peel the picture away like a turned page, or break it apart on the screen. With the touch of a button, these highly trained technicians can change the picture being transmitted. Of course, with the touch of the wrong button, they can put the wrong picture on the air and wreck a program. It is a tough, high-tension job.

The audio operator is in charge of the sound of the news program. He turns the microphones on and off and feeds the output to the air, riding the level to make sure it is not too loud or distorted. A mistake by the audio operator is usually a catastrophe. Imagine, for example, what would happen if someone's microphone were opened (turned on) at the wrong time. In 2006, Boston's WCVB-TV executives banned swearing in the newsroom after the "f-bomb" made it into one of their newscasts. It happened when the station broke in to carry a live press conference on the death of a University of Vermont student. During that segment, as the Burlington, Vermont, police chief spoke, a WCVB producer could be heard shouting the "F" word in the background.

In 2005, reporter Arthur Chi'en was fired by a CBS station in New York after hurling the "F"-word at a pair of hecklers during a live shot.

CNN anchor Kyra Phillips thought her microphone was off when she went into the ladies' room while President Bush delivered a speech in August 2006. Phillips chatted about her husband and called her sister-in-law a "control freak." CNN later apologized. We assume Kyra later apologized to her sister-in-law.

When Kathleen Sullivan was a host of *CBS This Morning*, she was on the set for a closed-circuit feed and did not realize her microphone was open. Her comments, referring to her employer, CBS, as the "cheap broadcasting system," went over the air and became a cause célèbre.

Microphone mistakes are not limited to the studio. At a 2000 Labor Day event in Naperville, Illinois, apparently oblivious of the microphone just inches from his mouth, Texas governor George W. Bush made a crude offhand remark about a *New York Times* reporter. Waving and smiling to the crowds, Bush spotted the reporter. He leaned across to tell his running mate, former defense secretary Dick Cheney, "There's Adam Clymer, major league a——hole from the *New York Times*."

Besides audio and pictures, words on the screen are still an important element on television news. They help identify people, places, and dates. These on-screen titles are usually formed by a computerized device called a character generator, such as the Chyron INFiNiT! The character generator operates like an electronic typewriter, printing titles on the screen. All the titles used in a newscast are usually prepared beforehand and stored in a computer for instant retrieval on the air. In February 2008 during the GOP primary race, Fox News identified John McCain as a Democrat in its Chyron. The type under his picture read "John McCain, D-AZ." *The Huffington Post* Web site noticed that McCain was under attack at the time by some Republicans who thought he was not conservative enough, and questioned whether the Chyron "error" was actually a mistake.

The still store / Chyron operator keeps track of "CGs" and graphics, and electronically produces them on the air when the director calls for them. Graphics include maps and drawings, often positioned over the shoulder of the anchor. They are supposed to illustrate what the story is about. For example, a story about a murder may be represented by the outline of a body and a gun. These graphics are created by artists who make them with computer imaging. In the early days of television, a graphic had to be drawn, then photographed (and the resulting slide projected behind the anchor). Now the graphic is produced, stored, and displayed entirely by computer.

The lighting director's function is to make sure the sets are illuminated properly, especially to show off the anchors to their best advantage. They monitor light meters and other equipment, and make adjustments as needed.

The remote coordinator is responsible for arranging microwave and satellite hookups to get on-the-air audio and video from outside the studio. She might arrange for a satellite link thousands of miles away or a microwave link around the corner. Each must get on the air without a glitch, if possible.

While computers have revolutionized most broadcast functions, they have not replaced makeup artists, who work to make everyone on the air look as good as possible. Using a magic box of tricks and cosmetics, the makeup person can take years off the face of an anchor, remove pounds from round faces, and even give a balding anchor the appearance of a man who needs his hair cut.

All of these people operating behind the scenes work to put the newscast on the air. But the meat and potatoes of the newscast is the gathering, preparing, and presentation of the news. Foremost among those responsible for the news is the news director, who hires and fires personnel and who sets the policy and the tone for the news department. We will deal with the news director in detail in the next chapter. Here we need only say that the people who carry out the news director's policy include the assistant news director and the managing editor, who make spot decisions on what events to cover. The producer decides what stories go into a program, which tape is used, the order of the stories, and the time each will be allocated. The executive producer is responsible for the overall product.

The assignment editors assign reporters to cover specific stories. Desk assistants, often an entry position, assist the "desk" responsible for covering the news of the day. Production assistants help with the behind-the-scenes nuts and bolts of the broadcast. They may locate and edit tapes or put scripts together. News editors wade through reams of stories from various sources and channel potential items to the producer.

The style of the newscast is often molded by the writing. Writers take facts and transform them into stories, trying to tell them in an interesting, accurate way. Copy from the wire services—facts from reporters and other sources—are the grist for the writer's mill. The craft of the writer is put to the test because each story must conform to the needs of television news. In some cases, complex stories must be compressed and told in fifteen or twenty seconds (which means a story will lose all context and nuance). Stories have to be written in the "voice" of the reader, tailor-made for the anchor's style and pace. Introductions to taped pieces and live shots have to set up the material properly and are usually written under great pressure. Videotape editors cut or edit, the raw tape or digital images into broadcast bites, clips, and B-roll (video for voice-overs). Librarians research facts and dig up needed footage that is filed in a tape room. In addition to these people, there are additional technicians, security guards, telephone operators, mail-room employees, interns, and others whose efforts contribute to the newscast eventually broadcast.

What you see on television news can, at times, be a free-flowing, extemporaneous, live experience. But the average prepackaged news story or documentary is anything but that. The packages are put together frame by frame, phrase by phrase, with hundreds of cuts or edits, stringing together image after image until the piece is completed. A good news package, like any good storytelling, tends to have a beginning, middle, and end, with seamless, flowing connections. Accomplishing this requires people who have been trained in the arts and crafts of camera work, writing, editing, narrating, and journalism.

Now that you have some sense of who does what, let's follow an item and see how it gets on a news broadcast. It's four o'clock in the afternoon, and eight-year-old Jimmy Barker sees smoke and fire coming from a downtown building. He tells his mother, who phones the fire department. Another witness phones the television station and talks to a telephone operator, who connects her to the newsroom. There, a desk assistant takes the call and advises the assignment editor of the details. The assignment editor calls the fire department for confirmation and additional information. She is told that an office building is on fire at 4567 Broadway. No further information is available.

The assignment editor figures that there could be many people in the building and advises the managing editor, who orders the desk to contact a reporter and crew by cell phone or two-way radio, sending them to the scene. The managing editor then asks the desk assistant to work the phones, in this case using a cross-reference phone book that lists phone numbers according to the address. The desk assistant calls a listing for the burning building, and someone answers the phone and says he is trapped with six other employees in his sixteenth-floor office. The smoke, he says, is too heavy for them to make their way down the stairs, and the elevators are not running. The desk assistant advises the managing editor of this. The story is shaping up as a major event. A reporter or producer does a recorded interview with the trapped person, and, as more confirming information comes in, the managing editor calls the news director. Together they decide that a helicopter should be chartered, and a crew and reporter are dispatched to get the view from the air.

In addition, a "live" truck is ordered to the scene. Its crew will race to the location and find a position where it can send a signal back to the station via microwave. It will raise an antenna and run a cable from the truck to a camera to record pictures of the burning building. In some cases, the camera can microwave its pictures back to the truck, wirelessly. The truck is self-contained; that is, it makes its own power and has the necessary cameras, recorders, monitors, and microwave transmitting equipment to send pictures back to the television station and if necessary "go live." It may even have editing equipment for on-the-go package production.

The reporter on the scene locates a command post set up by the fire department, and there he confirms that there are many people trapped in the building. Fire officials say the blaze seems to be located in the basement. The reporter radios this information back to the newsroom and begins debriefing eyewitnesses, interviewing them on tape as the story unfolds. The producer alerts the newsroom personnel that a major story is developing and will probably be the show lead. He is told a chopper is in the air, and there is the possibility of a live shot for the show. The wire services are now reporting the fire, and the writers and editors are reading the copy. A report indicates there have been some deaths, and the news director decides to go with the story at the top of the show.

The graphics department is now told that it should compose a graphic indicating fire in a high-rise. Engineering is advised to stand by for pictures from the live truck and the helicopter. The desk continues to work the phones, getting information that is relayed to the reporters. (Interestingly, the reporters who are in the middle of the action often find themselves isolated from the information flowing into the newsroom from all sources.) The reporters continue to record interviews with survivors and get pictures of people being carried out on stretchers, smoke pouring from the building, and flames shooting from windows, as firefighting equipment and ambulances jam the area. The assignment editor sends a courier to take a field producer to the scene and to return with tape or disc for a writer, who is assigned to screen and edit it with a technician.

As airtime approaches, the reporter at the scene is told he will lead the show and go live with a taped donut. He will then "throw" to the reporter in the helicopter, who will describe the scene from the air while the airborne cameraperson transmits pictures back. The engineering department assigns channels for the incoming signals. At airtime, the newscast begins with the anchor telling the audience about the fire, then introducing the reporter on the scene—the broadcast is off and running. The question of why this is news and why it should be the lead are easy to answer. Informing the community could help them stay alive. They may live in an adjacent building. They may have loved ones in the building. They may need to avoid driving in the area to allow emergency vehicles through or to avoid traffic delays. Audiences like to see fires: fires kill, and when people are killed there is drama. And, of course, this is live: it is happening, and it creates a sense of urgency and excitement. If it should turn out that the fire was started by an arsonist, the story will take on additional meaning. If it was an act of God, well, then the story demonstrates the fragility and unpredictability of human life. In any event, it is good television.

News producers and directors may be powerful people, but even they cannot make all the news happen live precisely when a newscast is on the air. So most stories have to be packaged in advanced, and indeed, as mentioned, they are even called packages. Let us take, as an example, an antipollution demonstration that occurs early in the morning. The event will have to be covered on tape. The assignment editor will send a reporter and a crew to the scene. When portable video-recording equipment was first used, one person would carry the deck (the recording and playback machine) and another person would operate the video camera. Sometimes a third person would handle the lights and audio. But in these days of miniaturized technology and cost consciousness, one-person camera crews are common. In any case, the crew arrives on the scene and shoots pictures of the speakers, the crowd, the signboards, the chanting, as well as a wide shot, showing the size of the crowd, and close-ups of faces. The camera will shoot from the podium, then from the point of view (POV) of the demonstrators. The raw video is called A-roll or B-roll. A-roll is the primary footage and includes elements such as on-camera reports, interviews, and primary scenes of the action with natural sound. B-roll, as mentioned, is the alternate footage shot to intercut with the primary shots used in a piece and is frequently used for cutaways. B-roll should be varied enough to show the action and give the editor something to work with.

The reporter will direct the cameraperson to get shots that will tell the story as the reporter sees it. If, for example, the reporter wishes to tell the story from the point of view of one of the protesters who lost her job when a polluting factory was closed down, the protester will be interviewed along with other people who agree and disagree with her. For additional B-roll, the reporter will ask the cameraperson to pan (smoothly move the camera laterally) from the protesters to the factory that closed down.

With the B-roll and interviews completed, the reporter will do "stand-ups." The reporter appears on camera introducing and/or linking parts of the story together and/or giving a conclusion to the piece. For dramatic effect, the reporter may want to have a picture of the swelling crowd behind him as he does his closing stand-up. In that case, he may have to tape his concluding remarks before the story is actually over.

Technically, in the field all material is recorded either electromagnetically on cassette tapes or digitally on optical disc, tape, or on the camera's hard drive. Before editing, the reporter will play the tape, disc, etc. and take notes. The final "shot sheet" will inventory the scenes, indicating when each takes place according to the electronic time code recorded by the camera. It looks sometimes like this:

:00	Crowd
:15	CU sign (CU = close-up)
:27	CU faces in crowd
1:46	Mayor Pentle speaks
2:30	Pan of crowd (pan = shot moving laterally)
3:20	Smoke stack (tilt), etc.
	(tilt = shot moving from bottom to top, or top to bottom)

This shot sheet will guide the reporter and editor as they put together a piece for the air. Basically, they will take a reporter or writer's script and put pictures to it. First the reporter narrates the script leading up to the first interview or "sound on tape" (SOT). Then each picture, or shot, is put in place, one after another. In an analog newsroom, each shot from the field tape is dubbed onto a master tape, one by one. If you're working on a digital system, each shot is downloaded directly onto a newsroom computer system one after another. Whatever format, the story might start by showing a pan of the protest signs (matching the voice-over) then the crowd, a close-up of a protest sign, the mayor speaking, and faces in the crowd. These shots are located and arranged in their new sequence. Natural sound on the tape may be used. When picture and sound are assembled, the story, made up of dozens of edits, is complete.

Usually, the finished story ("piece") is around two minutes long. The reporter may then write a suggested lead to guide the writer who prepares the anchor's introduction to the piece. The reporter must also make a list of the names and titles of the people interviewed for the story, in the order and noting the time they appear on the screen. These, along with dates and locations, will be generated on the screen to help identify them. A two-minute package may represent a full day's work by a reporter and the labors of a half-dozen technicians. And there will be four to six such pieces in the average half-hour newscast.

As the elements of the news program are assembled, the producer decides where each of the stories (scripted and taped) will go. Writers have written the scripts including lead-ins to taped stories and eyeball stories (those read by the anchor without tape) as well as stories for which the anchor will provide voice-over for the pictures. Before broadcast time, the anchors read over the scripts. The director and technical staff review the necessary information explaining the order, source, and length of each story. And the show is on the air.

As for the story of the antipollution rally, there will have been little time to explain to the audience what an antipollution rally means. How, for example, did these people get organized? What are the scientific arguments for and against the dangers of pollution in this case? How many other antipollution rallies have been held in this region? Who owns the company that is accused of polluting the environment? What is the position of the local political leaders on this question? And so on. As we have said, television news is in a constant struggle with time, and time is a fierce adversary. Two minutes for the antipollution rally—that's it. And plenty of pictures. Moreover, as we have tried to suggest in this chapter, the technical demands of television are so complex and unrelenting that everyone concerned is preoccupied with getting matters technically right. Frequently, it is a case of technique triumphing over substance. In TV news, that is the way it goes most of the time.

CHAPTER 6

The News Director

EARLIER, WE DISCUSSED THE question "What is news?" We said that viewers must consider this question seriously, with a view toward finding answers that express their social and political, not to mention spiritual, values. But to most working TV journalists, the answer to the question is moot. For them, the news is determined by what the news director thinks is important and, of course, will draw an audience. In the previous chapter, we mentioned the news director. Here we need to say more about these executives since their decisions do much to form our consciousness of what the world is like.

Perhaps the first thing to be said about news directors is that they usually don't last long at their jobs. In fact, they tell a story among themselves that aptly describes their burden. It goes like this:

A news director has been fired. He tells the incoming news director that he has left behind three envelopes, each one to be opened after a ratings period. The news show does very poorly in the first "sweeps" period, and the new news director goes to the desk and opens the first envelope. It reads, "Fire the anchors." When the news director is called to the general manager's office to explain what is wrong with the news department, he answers, "Fire the anchors." The general manager nods in agreement and fires the anchors. The next sweeps period is even worse. Once again the news director is summoned to the general manager's office. Before going in, he remembers the envelopes and opens the second one. It says, "Change the set." When the general manager asks the news director what is wrong with the news department, the news director replies, "We need a new set." The general manager agrees. But the new set doesn't help the ratings either, and the next sweeps period is a catastrophe. The news director goes to his desk and opens the last envelope. It reads, "Take three envelopes and . . ."

The Radio-Television News Directors Association reports that the average time a news director stays at the same job is 3.4 years; the median is just 2 years. The reason for the revolving door is the enormous pressure on them to excel, not in the journalistic arena, but in ratings.

This does not mean that news directors have no attachment to the traditions of journalism. Most news directors value truth, speed, and accuracy, and they have well-developed ideas about what is important. But their jobs depend on how many people watch their shows. So they need help. "Help," in this case, is a rather ambiguous term. What the general manager or the sales department of a station considers help may not be what the news director considers help. For example, take the case of news consultants.

Consultants are hired by stations to find ways to increase the ratings of news shows and to do so quickly. The usual way to proceed is by emphasizing "hair-spray ethics" at the expense of solid journalism. Consultants, therefore, may not be interested in or knowledgeable about journalism. They can say if an "on-air talent" is likable and a "good communicator" but are usually unqualified to judge the quality of news reports. The methods of consultants differ from company to company and from station to station. But basically, they look at the news programs and recommend ways of attracting more viewers—that is to say, customers—to it. It's that simple.

For example, using techniques of market research, a consultant may draw a profile of the average viewer the station wants to attract. The profile is a statistical compilation of, among other things, the age, economic status, and consumer habits of the audience. The consultant then carefully observes the anchors and reporters to determine if they fit the viewer profile. Do these viewers like to watch these anchors and reporters? To assist in answering this question, a consultant may form a focus group to get the reaction of "average" viewers to the anchors and reporters, as well as to their potential replacements. A focus group is nothing more than a collection of representative viewers who watch tapes of programs under controlled conditions and report their reactions. Consultants rely heavily on focus groups because it is difficult to guess what audiences will like or hate. It is best to ask "average" viewers and extrapolate from there. The issue can be quite complicated. Male viewers, for example, may not like a certain female anchor, believing her to be too aggressive. Women viewers may find a female anchor too seductive. Men may like a certain male anchor because of his authority; women may dislike the same anchor for the same reason. To feed the focus groups, major consulting firms such as Frank Magid Associates in Marion, Iowa, have huge computerized files with videos of almost every on-air reporter in the country. If a consultant recommends a blond, blue-eyed, twenty-seven-year-old female reporter with five years' experience, chances are there's one in the file.

In addition to focus groups, consultants frequently depend on track records; that is, how an anchor or reporter has performed in the ratings in the past. The theory is that if an anchor has done well in one market, he or she will "travel" well and get good ratings in another market. The theory does not always fit the facts. There are many cases of anchors who have been unable to duplicate their ratings success from one market to another. But obviously some anchors can bring their popularity with them, and indeed that is their main talent.

What all of this means is that consultants may be able to help a news director keep his or her job. Or may not. But it is clear that consultants usually are not competent to help the news director in deciding what is worth reporting. For this, most news directors rely on fairly traditional sources.

For example, many story ideas originate in newspapers, which traditionally have larger staffs and more beat reporters than TV stations. Newspaper headline stories are developed and reported on the evening news by general-assignment reporters. Other story ideas come from the police and fire department radio reports of crimes, fires, and accidents. Viewers sometimes phone in news tips. And, of course, staff members may develop stories based on their own observations. For example, a reporter might notice that a department store isn't too crowded during a normally busy season. That might be an indication that the local economy is on a downswing. There could be a story in that. Or a reporter, noticing that there are extra men in the mayor's security force, may uncover news that a threat has been made on the mayor's life. Many stories are originated by press secretaries and public relations firms issuing press releases ("handouts") to the news media.

And, of course, some news has such great impact that it determines the news director's selection. According to the *Tyndall Report*, the attacks of September 11, 2001, and the subsequent wars led to increased coverage of foreign policy and global conflict on the network evening news but decreased coverage of domestic issues. In the years 2002–05, the number of minutes devoted to foreign policy was up 102 percent, coverage of armed conflict rose 69 percent, and coverage of terrorism rose 135 percent. Coverage of domestic issues like crime and law enforcement dropped by half, as did coverage of science and technology.

Sometimes news comes in over the transom or, more accurately, via a download from a satellite in the form of video news releases, or VNRs. They can be tempting to the news director because the VNRs are free and come prepackaged, including a whole story ready for seamless insertion into a newscast. The complete "pseudonews" packages include "slates" (text about the story), a complete ready-to-air news package, some unedited sound bites, and B-roll (accompanying video). VNRs are created by public relations firms that specialize in broadcast. Although the accompanying information sent to the TV stations identifies the clients behind the VNRs, nothing in the video package does. Some TV news operations disguise the VNR segments as their own reporting despite FCC warnings. In September 2007, the FCC proposed to fine Comcast $4,000 for running VNRs without disclosing the provider. The FCC's enforcement division said Comcast's CN8 news channel, which is seen in twenty markets, including New York, Washington, and Philadelphia, ran most of a news release produced by D S Simon Productions for Nelson's Rescue Sleep, an herbal alternative to sleeping pills, on November 11, 2006. And the FCC indicated it was considering action on one hundred similar complaints. The VNR issue turned political shortly before the 2004 election when the Department of Health and Human Services produced a video news release for a Medicare prescription-drug benefit not due to take effect until 2005. Democrats charged that the video was a thinly veiled political ad for the Bush administration. The VNR aired on forty stations between January 22 and February 12, 2004. Public relations specialist and former television news reporter Karen Ryan produced the video news release and appears in it as a reporter hyping the government's Medicare program. The fake news story ends with her saying, "In Washington, this is Karen Ryan reporting." In May 2004, the Ryan VNR was ruled to be in violation of federal law by the Government Accountability Office (GAO), the investigative arm of the U.S. government. An investigation by the GAO concluded that the VNR had violated a ban on government-funded "publicity and propaganda."

Karen Ryan was back in the news in October 2004. This time Ryan "reported" on the Bush administration's No Child Left Behind Act. The U.S. Department of Education paid $700,000 to the PR firm to produce two VNRs. In September 2005, the GAO concluded that the Department of Education had violated the law when it distributed the No Child Left Behind VNR using Ryan as a "reporter." (On the subject of No Child Left Behind, the Education Department acknowledged paying commentator Armstrong Williams to promote the controversial policy. He touted the No Child Left Behind program to his radio and TV audiences without disclosing he was getting paid for his PR work.) The Center for Media and Democracy along with another group, Free Press, eventually filed complaints with the FCC about 111 TV stations and cable providers running video news releases without identification, including Comcast. The action against Comcast was the first response by the FCC to the complaints.

The VNR problem is not a new one. In its February 22, 1992, issue, *TV Guide* documented story after story in which video supplied by lobbying groups, product manufacturers,

and political candidates was used in news programs without labeling the source. The examples included a segment on the hazards of automatic safety belts in cars, a "story" run on the *CBS Evening News* on June 13, 1991. The tape showed a car being tipped on its side, the door opening, and the strap allowing a dummy to fall out and be crushed beneath the car. The casual viewer would assume the tape was shot by CBS News. But, in fact, it was prepared by the Institute for Injury Reduction, a lobbying group largely supported by lawyers whose clients often sue auto companies for crash-related injuries. According to Nielsen Media Research, by 1994 100 percent of TV stations were using VNRs, and 80 percent were doing so at least several times a month. The Center for Media and Democracy's senior researcher, Diane Farsetta, says there were 3,300 VNRs made available to news departments in 2006, at a fraction of the cost of a commercial. VNR-producer Medialink Worldwide says it can make a three-minute video news release for $15,000 to $25,000. A thirty-second TV commercial costs ten to twenty times more. With satellite-transponder time costing $250 to $500 per hour, many video releases will shower down from the heavens to more picture-hungry television news operations in the years to come.

Corporate America is not the only source of VNRs. In 2005, the *New York Times* revealed how the Bush administration has used prepackaged ready-to-serve news reports to promote its policies. The *Times* found that at least twenty federal agencies, including the Pentagon and the Census Bureau, have made and distributed hundreds of television news segments over the past four years. Many were subsequently broadcast on local stations across the country without any acknowledgement of the government's role in their production. In one VNR produced by the State Department, the narrator tells how after the collapse of Saddam Hussein's regime,

"In suburban Detroit, hundreds of Iraqi Americans marched triumphantly through the streets. The community of Dearborn is home to America's largest Arab community. On Warren Avenue people chanted, 'No more Saddam,' as they honked horns and waved Iraqi and American flags." This was followed by talking heads of Iraqi Americans extolling their appreciation for President Bush and the United States. In another example, a VNR financed by the Department of Health and Human Services was aired on a number of local news programs around the country as conventional journalism, when in fact it was produced to promote the new Medicare plan.

Of course, the number of press releases increases enormously during political campaigns and is supplemented by a deluge of "photo opportunities." In this situation, the print press and TV press are invited to "see all but speak not" to the candidate posing under the lights. Reporters usually ask questions anyway, and, typically, officials who do not wish to answer pretend they don't know what has been asked. "Sorry, Sam. I can't hear you."

The photo op is, obviously, a particularly important source of news for television. In America, politicians are largely known by their image on television. As a consequence, politicians like to do things that show them in a positive light: visiting a hospital, welcoming a visitor from another country, observing the aftermath of a train wreck, and so on. News directors accommodate the visual needs of politicians because television needs pictures. There is not much television news to be made of a congressman's twenty-two-page position paper on the decline of education in a particular city. But a photo op of the congressman inspecting a decaying building is useful.

What was once viewed as a premier presidential photo op has continued to haunt President George W. Bush. On May 1, 2003, the president landed on an aircraft carrier in the copilot's seat of a Navy S–3B Viking after making two flybys of the carrier USS *Abraham Lincoln*. He was there to declare "one victory" in the war on terrorism and an end to major combat operations in Iraq. Behind President Bush when he gave the speech was a giant "Mission Accomplished" sign—a photo op if you ever saw one. But the mission was far from accomplished. After the "victory" speech, U.S. casualties in Iraq continued to rise; the war got more intense and was still raging four years later.

A considerable number of events are staged to attract television cameras. When a political candidate goes to a closed factory or stands outside slums so a camera can capture the scene, he or she is manipulating television coverage. For example, President Ronald Reagan's 1985 visit to a cemetery in Bitburg, Germany, was arranged so that photographers were forced to shoot from positions that prevented them from getting both the president and the grave sites of Nazi Waffen SS soldiers in a single frame. Some people get so good at figuring out how to do this kind of thing that they get paid for it. Of course, they are not called manipulators. They are called political consultants.

Before Roger Ailes became the chairman and CEO of Fox News, he ran the Bush media campaign in 1988. Ailes claims that three things always get covered by television: visuals, attacks, and mistakes. Despite the networks spending about $30 million each to cover presidential political campaigns, NBC News chief foreign affairs correspondent Andrea Mitchell thinks political strategists and consultants are learning to manipulate television too effectively, staging events and orchestrating sound bites and photo ops to promote their candidates. She quotes Larry Speakes, Ronald Reagan's press secretary, as saying to the news media, "Don't tell us how to stage the news, and we won't tell you how to cover it." Mitchell believes that managed television news coverage has made it difficult for reporters to provide the necessary scrutiny of presidents in office or presidential candidates because deadlines, competition, and limited access make meaningful coverage close to impossible. Mitchell asks, "Aside from pictures, what do we remember from the last campaign? We remember the battle of sound bites, those snappy one-liners like 'Read my lips, no new taxes.' " She laments that "the average sound bite has shrunk, from forty-five seconds ten years ago, to fifteen seconds in 1985, to nine seconds in the '88 campaign." According to a study by the Center for Media and Public Affairs, the average length of sound bites by presidential candidates on the network nightly news has dropped to 7.3 seconds, a 26 percent decline since 1988 (9.8 seconds) and 83 percent since the 1968 presidential election. It makes you wonder just what a candidate can tell a voter in so little time.

Former CBS legal correspondent Fred Graham reports that back in 1975, when Richard Salant and Walter Cronkite dominated CBS News, the average sound bite ran sixteen seconds. Ten years later, when Van Gordon Sauter and Dan Rather were the dominating forces, the average length of a sound bite in one of Graham's pieces was nine seconds. Graham complains that some sound bites that survived the editing process were so short as to defy understanding. Two independent studies since the 1968 election confirm the trend. Kiku Adatto, a Harvard University sociologist, and Daniel Hallin, a University of California at San Diego political scientist, both showed that sound bites of presidential candidates on the network evening news had shrunk by more than 75 percent between 1968 and 1988. Dr. Hallin argues that one gains a broader understanding of a candidate's character and the logic of his or her argument in a paragraph than in a ten-second sound bite. That is, when a sound bite is even presented on the news. An October 2006

University of Wisconsin study found that Midwest TV stations gave short shrift to election issues. The study of nine midwestern markets showed that TV stations devoted an average of thirty-six seconds—that's right, seconds—per 30 minutes of news to election issues in the thirty days following the traditional Labor Day campaign kickoff. That, compared to 10 minutes of advertising, 7 minutes of sports and weather, and 2.5 minutes of crime stories.

With reduced TV news coverage, candidates get their message across effectively by paying for it. According to figures released by the Alliance for Better Campaigns, candidates, parties, and independent groups spent more than $1.6 billion on television ads in 2004, a record for any campaign year and double the amount spent in the 2000 presidential election.

News directors are, of course, aware of all this; indeed, most of them probably disapprove of photo ops, sound bites, and staged events. But they are in a competitive business, under pressure from executive producers, sales managers, and sponsors to draw audiences. And they can never forget that lurking in their desks is the envelope that prophesizes their end. So news directors will not disregard staged events, not even those that appear in the "daybook."

The daybook is, in fact, a major source of television stories. Daybook items are listings of scheduled events, including official functions such as press conferences and ceremonies at city hall, press agents' creations (e.g., Lucille Ball look-alike contests), and activities that are supposed to be spontaneous but often are not (e.g., protests and demonstrations). In setting up the daily news "budget" the news director and the managing editor often make assignments from the daybook. And a good news director understands that on a slow Sunday in August a photo opportunity of Miss Coney Island sitting on a cold block of ice might make an item on the eleven o'clock news.

From what we have said so far, you will conclude correctly that the task of the news director is extremely complex. Multiple decisions must be made, taking into account not only the question "What is news?" but, more important, "What is television news?" And while on any given day most of the audience accepts without complaint the wisdom of the news director's decisions, there are groups of people who monitor these decisions almost daily, to determine if they are being fairly treated or if the news director's decisions have violated some political or social ideal. They are called watchdog groups, and from the point of view of a news director, they are little else but an unwanted complication.

These groups have a wide range of interests, from Democrats who believe they're getting less airtime than Republicans to fundamentalists checking for on-air obscenities. They are not reluctant to make their views known or to try to bring pressure on programmers to change the content of shows. For example, the nonprofit, Web-based Media Matters for America argues that the Sunday-morning talk shows on ABC, CBS, and NBC are where prevailing opinions in American politics are supposed to be aired and tested, with both the left and right, debating the pressing issues of the day on equal ground. But Media Matters says conservative voices significantly outnumber progressive voices on the Sunday talk shows. It conducted a content analysis of ABC's *This Week*, CBS's *Face the Nation*, and NBC's *Meet the Press*, classifying each of the nearly seven thousand guest appearances during Bill Clinton's second term, George W. Bush's first term, and the year 2005 as either Democrat, Republican, conservative, progressive, or neutral. The watchdog group says the conclusion is clear: Republicans and conservatives have been offered more opportunities to appear on the Sunday shows and, in some cases, dramatically so.

Among the study's key findings:

➤ During President Bush's first term, Republicans/conservatives held a dramatic advantage, outnumbering Democrats/progressives 58 percent to 42 percent. In 2005, the figures were identical: 58 percent to 42 percent.

➤ During both the Clinton and Bush administrations, conservative journalists were far more likely to appear on the Sunday shows than progressive journalists.

➤ In every year examined by the study (1997–2005), more panels tilted right (a greater number of Republicans/conservatives than Democrats/progressives) than tilted left. In some years, there were two, three, or even four times as many right-titled panels as left-tilted panels.

➤ Congressional opponents of the Iraq war were largely absent from the Sunday shows, particularly during the period just before the war began.

In short, Media Matters concluded that the Sunday talk shows on ABC, CBS, and NBC are dominated by conservative voices, from newsmakers to commentators.

An earlier study, in 1989, by a liberal watchdog group called Fairness and Accuracy in Reporting (FAIR) criticized the *MacNeil/Lehrer NewsHour* and *Nightline,* claiming that the programs have a white-male, conservative leaning. Naturally, the shows defended themselves. *MacNeil/Lehrer* executive producer Les Crystal pointed out that FAIR failed to take into account the lengthy tape reports that are a significant part of the program. As to the predominance of white males, well (the defense goes), most officials in American politics *are* white males. If FAIR had studied the interviews of and reports about professional basketball players, it would have found that 70 percent or more featured black males. More recently, in 2006, in the PBS "Ombudsman Column," Michael Getler pointed to viewer criticism about a segment on *The News-Hour with Jim Lehrer* dealing with oil giant British Petroleum (BP) shutting down production in its Prudhoe Bay, Alaska, oil field because of badly corroded pipelines that had not been properly maintained for many years. The program host introduced the segment, stating for the record that BP is a *News-Hour* underwriter. Some viewers felt the segment hadn't probed deep enough into the what they saw as "the real story of BP's negligence." Our point is not about the reporting of the BP story itself but that corporate underwriting may leave a negative impression in the minds of some PBS viewers and watchdog organizations.

Sometimes, despite watchdog groups, news directors make more news by manipulating bad press. In November 2006, Fox said it would air an interview with O. J. Simpson in which he describes the 1994 murders of his ex-wife and her friend. The interview would be conducted by publisher Judith Regan, who supposedly paid more than $3 million for Simpson's book *If I Did It, Here's How It Happened*. Rupert Murdoch owned both the book publisher, Regan Books, and Fox television. The story, which CBS News anchor Bob Schieffer called the most disgusting story of the year, played high on Fox TV newscasts. In August 2007, the book was awarded to the parents of one of the victims, Ron Goldman, by a Florida bankruptcy court in connection with an unpaid civil judgment they won in their wrongful-death suit against Simpson.

Watchdog groups serve as a feedback mechanism, forcing producers and news directors to defend their decisions and, sometimes, to alter their habitual ways of thinking. On the other hand, sensitivity to feedback can produce responses aimed at minimizing economic damage. Networks and syndicators with an eye on sponsors' satisfaction and stockholders' dividends are particularly fearful about charges concerning their talent. In October 2004, a female Fox News producer claimed that Bill O'Reilly subjected her to repeated instances of sexual harassment. She sued and the case was quietly settled. In February 1990, Andy Rooney was suspended by CBS, accused of making a racist remark in a magazine interview. A public uproar ensued. The fact that Rooney denied the charge and had been an honored employee with forty years' experience did not prevent the network from suspending him from the popular program *60 Minutes*. The program's ratings dropped, and the network, apparently fearing economic consequences, reinstated Rooney.

But the incident demonstrates two important points. First, TV executives are hypersensitive to public criticism. Second, a principal consideration in responding to public criticism is profit and loss. The news director who arranges matters so that public criticism is kept to a minimum and profits remain high, does not have to open the last envelope in the desk drawer.

CHAPTER 7

Reenactments and Docudramas, or No News Is Still News

O N SEVERAL OCCASIONS, FORMER president Ronald Reagan enjoyed telling how he re-created Chicago Cubs games in his years as a baseball announcer. In the early days of radio, details of baseball games were telegraphed down the line to radio stations, where announcers would re-create the game without seeing it. When the information was slow in coming, the announcers were forced to use their imaginations to fill in the details. They would, for example, describe how the pitcher was taking his time, was picking up the resin bag and checking the new ball thrown to him by the umpire. In other words, the announcer would kill time until the telegraph details started flowing again. What the announcer said might not have been the truth, but it was good theater. To make even better theater, the announcer would hit a stick against piece of wood to simulate the sound of a bat hitting a ball. It sounded real but it wasn't. It was a baseball game imagined by the announcer. A re-creation. We might say, a "docudrama."

Re-creations were used from time to time on radio programs other than baseball games. For example, the program *The*

March of Time was a form of docudrama employing actors who impersonated historic figures such as Hitler, Churchill, and Roosevelt. The tradition carried over to television. On *60 Minutes*, for example, actors use stage accents to make believe they are interpreters. *You Are There* aired from 1953 to 1957 and again, for one season, in 1971. Its host was Walter Cronkite. The program re-created various historical events complete with conversations no one had ever heard. To his credit, Cronkite is on record as believing that historical re-creations have "no place in a news division," that, in effect, they are to be used to entertain and not for anything else.

But that was long ago, before the line separating news and entertainment became blurred, before news programming became a cash cow. Television's need to fill the blank screen brought re-creations back in ways that might have even surprised Ronald Reagan. Instead of an anchor simply talking about an event on camera, reenactments allow actors and other masters of stagecraft to formulate scenes that approximate events from the past. Instead of a blank screen, we have a simulation of reality—a reenactment.

Generally speaking, television executives don't see reenactments as a problem, primarily because reenactments make engrossing television. But some critics claim that re-creations mislead the viewer into thinking he or she is watching a recording of the real thing. When cameras were banned at Michael Jackson's child-molestation trial in 2005, an American and a British television company got together, figuring if they couldn't have the real thing they'd fake it. E! Entertainment Television and satellite company British Sky Broadcasting (BSkyB) used actors to present daily recreations of the trial. By 2007, CBS News' *48 Hours Mystery*, NBC News' *Dateline NBC*, and ABC News' *Primetime* all used reenactments regularly. Perhaps the most famous example of a re-creation gone astray took place in July 1989. ABC's *World News Tonight* showed footage of U.S. diplomat Felix Bloch handing a briefcase to a Soviet agent. The scene was not labeled as a re-creation. The word "simulation" or some other warning, such as "what you are seeing, we made up," was accidentally left off the screen, leaving viewers with the impression they were watching the actual taped event. The entire scene was broadcast for only ten seconds, but its impact was great. It focused attention on the problem inherent in "re-creating" reality.

These problems do not disappear even when a recreation is properly labeled. For example, the CBS series *Saturday Night with Connie Chung* presented the story of Abbie Hoffman's last days. Hoffman, after a colorful career as an activist for various causes, committed suicide. The program purported to reveal the last moments of Hoffman's life. His last words, reenacted, were as follows:

> ABBIE: I'm okay, Jack. I'm okay. Yeah, I'm out of bed. I got my feet on the floor. Yeah. Two feet. I'll see you Wednesday? Thursday. I'll always be with you, Jack. Don't worry.

Viewers knew, of course, that Hoffman was already dead, so they could not be hearing his last words as he spoke them. But many believed, and had a right to believe, that someone had recorded the event and that these were Hoffman's actual words. They weren't. They were words pieced together by interviews and then scripted by a writer. Does it matter that the words attributed to Abbie Hoffman in his last moments were never uttered?

Some say it doesn't. In fact, besides using recreations for short segments on news shows, TV producers have created whole programs of simulated reality. They are called docudramas. These usually use real news stories as the story line's starting point, then weave in events created by a writer. CBS had a docudrama called *The Reagans* ready to roll in 2003 when conservative political din forced CBS to cancel the show and hand it off to Showtime, the cable outlet of its parent company, Viacom. CBS chairman Les Moonves told a Yale University audience that he did not drop *The Reagans* because of political or advertiser pressure but because he felt the docudrama was too "biased" against the Reagans for CBS. In one example, according to a script posted by Showtime, the docudrama shows Reagan losing his faculties almost as soon as he became president. In reality, he was diagnosed with Alzheimer's disease in 1995, more than five years after leaving office.

In 2006, another docudrama came under attack when former president Bill Clinton blasted the ABC production *The Path to 9/11* for being inaccurate and unfair. His major complaint involved a scene where his security adviser Richard Clarke (played by Stephen Root) stops the CIA from assassinating Osama bin Laden out of concern that the president wants to avoid political damage in case the mission goes badly. That scene cut to real footage of Clinton testifying that "I did not have sexual relations with that woman, Monica Lewinsky." The implication was that President Clinton did not pull the trigger on bin Laden because he was too preoccupied with his political troubles. Another scene in question supposedly portrays Madeleine Albright refusing to shoot missiles at Osama bin Laden without authority from Pakistan and eventually getting "permission" from them against the military's wishes. Albright insists that this is a falsity and completely inaccurate. The extent of the criticism and indignation expressed led to ABC revising its original description of the film as a "docudrama based on the 9/11 commission report" to calling it a dramatization of events based only in part on the 9/11 commission report. The scriptwriter for the film, Cyrus Nowrasteh, was asked if he thought of the script as a "historical document," and he responded: "No, but I stand by the original version of the movie, and I stand by the edited version. . . . There has to be conflation of events. The most obvious problem any dramatist faces is that of sheer length. I had to collapse the events of eight and a half years into five hours. I don't know any other way to do it except collapse, conflate, and condense." On September 10, 2006, part one aired on ABC. According to *Editor & Publisher* magazine, when compared with the review copy in its possession, less than one minute had been "cropped out." All the controversial scenes were included in some manner, with only brief shots trimmed and occasional word substitutions made. In addition, a written and spoken disclaimer was aired at the beginning and end of the movie, as well as just past the midpoint of the first evening's broadcast, reminding viewers that the movie was a fictionalization.

The events in docudramas may or may not be true, but producers defend them by arguing that the audience understands it is not watching the actual event. The fact that studies show that audiences tend to absorb information from television even though they forget where that information originated does not trouble producers of docudramas.

Producers like docudramas for a variety of reasons. For one thing, they take the form of a theatrical event with a beginning, middle, and end, with time-outs for commercials. Actual news events, of course, are not always so tidy. In real-life dramas, heroes get killed, hostages are sometimes not released, and the villain is not always brought to justice. Most newsworthy events are not concluded in neat thirty- or sixty-minute segments. A docudrama can remedy unhappy or unjust conclusions by packaging them in palatable forms.

Another reason some producers like docudramas is their low cost. A re-created one-hour news docudrama might cost $400,000 to $500,000, at least half the cost of a similar theatrical drama using popular actors, good writers, scenic designers, and directors. Full-length, made-for-TV docudramas are produced at a fraction of the cost of a theatrical movie: $3 million to $5 million versus $25 million to $40 million.

In 2004, Deborah Potter, executive director of Newslab, a broadcast training and research center, and a former network correspondent, published an article called "Viewer Beware" in the *American Journalism Review*. She warned about the dangers of stations reenacting scenes, adding sounds, and using other misleading practices. She explained that during the November 2005 sweeps period, for example, three Memphis stations aired re-creations of crime stories. One station did it more than once and didn't always bother to let viewers in on the practice.

KLAS-TV in Las Vegas obtained security-camera video of a casino robbery in which a gambler was killed and a security guard wounded. The footage was silent, of course, but that didn't stop the station from adding sounds of slot machines and gunshots before airing it.

The lines between re-creations and reality are so muddled that some news programs have even used Hollywood films to illustrate news stories. There is nothing producers or news directors fear more than a void, a black hole in a newscast, as, for example, when the anchor is talking about a subject and there is no newsreel footage to go with the comments. What to do? On one CBS newscast, while Dan Rather reported on new exploration of the *Titanic* wreckage, the picture on the screen was from a movie depicting the sinking of the *Titanic*, complete with wet actors manning the lifeboats. It was enough to give serious journalists a sinking feeling. On *NBC Nightly*

News with Tom Brokaw, a reporter used footage from the movie *The Spy Who Came in from the Cold* to illustrate the changing role of the CIA in light of the Soviet Union's fading menace. The next logical step would be to run a clip of battle footage from a John Wayne movie when discussing fighting during World War II, or any war that happens to be around. To our knowledge, that hasn't happened—yet.

So where should the lines be drawn? Is it acceptable to add applause to footage of a concert or sirens to a police-car chase scene or gunfire to battle footage? Is it ethical for a television journalist to use a "reverse question"; that is, the technique of taking pictures of a reporter asking again the questions he used during an earlier interview, then splicing the footage into the finished tape? The "reverse" played a key role in the movie *Broadcast News* when a reporter used it to fake tears, trying to show how sensitive he was to the issue of date rape.

Edward R. Murrow once addressed these issues and made the following unambiguous remark: "There will always be some errors in news gathering, but the tricks that microphones, cameras, and film make possible must never be contrived to pass off as news events that were fabricated to document an event that we missed or which may never have happened."

Murrow is generally regarded as the man who established the standards of TV news, and we can assume his microphone would short out were he to know about the uses made of recreations today. Indeed, we can imagine he would have some harsh words for pseudonews shows such as *A Current Affair, Hard Copy,* or *Geraldo Rivera,* which were the rage in the eighties and nineties. Rivera's programs were not under the control of news departments but drew part of their appeal from the fact that they involved real people and real events. They were television's version of "yellow journalism," typically dealing with sensational, weird, or perverse stories. A recent example, under the banner of Fox News, is *Geraldo at Large*. In December 2006, programming featured "Trump vs. Rosie," "Porn Star Turned Teacher," "Cable Guy Murder," and "Santa Sex Offender."

The defense for this kind of programming proceeds along the following lines. First, it draws huge audiences, which suggests that people are interested in them. Second, the high profitability of the shows allows the hosts to include material devoted to more acceptable news content: an interview with the secretary of defense, for example, or a discussion of industrial pollution. The audience is attracted by the promise of the bizarre, and then exposed to serious issues. Third, programs about battered lesbians, girls who can't say no, and parents of slain prostitutes are news, and serious news at that. They tell as much, or more, about the state of our society as do 90 percent of the stories on any daily network news show. They are a form of documentary journalism; they reveal the pain, humiliation, and confusion of real people trying to cope with intractable realities.

The answer to these arguments is that such programming is nothing more than a highly profitable freak show, exploiting the insatiable curiosity of audiences for what is strange and forbidden. The audience members are voyeurs, peeking, as it were, into the bedrooms or living rooms of people who are desperately seeking a momentary sense of celebrity. Besides, such programs serve as a diversion from the urgent issues of the day. To borrow a phrase from Fred Friendly, formerly of CBS News: "What the American people don't know can kill them." To this might be added that what people *do* know can keep them from knowing what they *must* know. In other words, the pseudonews show fixes people's attention on what is peripheral to an understanding of their lives and may even disable them from distinguishing what is relevant from what is not.

In fact, a somewhat similar set of arguments is made against the docudramas and re-creations (especially those done within the context of news shows). It proceeds as follows: A re-creation can be as engrossing as a program about men who marry prostitutes. But while the latter diverts attention from what it is necessary to know, the former severs the trust that citizens must have in their sources of information. For example, consider the following December 11, 2006, *New York Times* story about the tsunami that hit Banda Aceh two years earlier: "The tsunami killed 170,000 people and left half a million homeless here in Aceh Province. Only 43,400 permanent homes have been built in the two years since the tsunami, but 128,000 are needed, according to the United Nations. Twelve thousand families remain in temporary accommodations."

Now, let's pretend that you learned that the *Times* story was in error: that only 50,000 people were killed and that it wasn't actually a tsunami but just a big wave. You would, we imagine, abandon whatever trust you have in the *New York Times* as a reliable source of news. We imagine further that you would not be impressed with an explanation claiming that the alterations were made to give the story more drama. Moreover, if you think our example exaggerates the extent to which a TV docudrama may depart from reality, we should observe that in an NBC miniseries depicting the life of Peter the Great there was a scene in which Peter meets with Isaac Newton, a meeting which never took place except in the imaginations of the program's writer, director, and producer. The two of them did live, roughly, at the same time: Peter died in 1725, Newton in 1727. Is this justification for a scene in which they have a conversation? Perhaps, if you take the view that all television is only a form of entertainment. Not at all, if you take the more rigorous position that when entertainment conflicts with truth, truth must prevail.

We must call attention to the fact that actors and sets are not necessary to create pseudonews. Sometimes bending the facts is enough to blow smoke at the truth. At times it's even laughable. On the *Today* show, in October 2005, Katie Couric was promoting a segment about an apparently staged interview with soldiers in Iraq. Moments later, the show switched to correspondent Michelle Kosinski, reporting on location about floods in New Jersey. Kosinski was in a canoe in what looked like deep water. But then, two men strolled into the frame of the TV picture, walking in what turned out to be a few inches of water. Kosinski attempted to brush it off, but Katie and Matt had a good laugh along with the rest of the audience.

Apparently, the U.S. military isn't adverse to manipulating the news media from time to time. On April 1, 2003, PFC Jessica Lynch became an icon of the Iraq war, an all-American hero. The military account told of the heroic rescue of nineteen-year-old Lynch after her convoy was ambushed when it took a wrong turn near Nassiriya. Nine of her comrades were killed, and Iraqi soldiers took Lynch to a local hospital where she was held for eight days. No one disputes that.

The Pentagon claimed that Lynch had stab and bullet wounds, that she had been slapped around on her hospital bed, and that she had been interrogated. The Pentagon says an Iraqi lawyer risked his life to alert the Americans that Lynch was being held. After midnight, Army Rangers and Navy SEALS stormed the hospital. The "daring" assault was captured on the military's night-vision camera. They were said to have come under fire but made it to Lynch and carried her away on a helicopter as she clutched an American flag. TV news carried the story extensively.

The Iraqi lawyer was granted asylum in the United States and got a $500,000 book deal to tell his story. The doctors at the hospital in Nassiriya said they remembered that they gave Lynch the best treatment available. The doctors say there were no signs of bullet or stab wounds, only injuries from a road-traffic accident, including broken bones. The doctors say the day before the "rescue" the Iraqi military had fled. And a doctor swears that two days before the "rescue" he tried to deliver Lynch to the Americans at a checkpoint in an ambulance, but the U.S. forces opened fire on the vehicle and it turned back. None of the doctors' stories made it into the TV news reports. Lynch said she couldn't remember anything about her ordeal. We should mention here that that ordeal was the subject of a docudrama, NBC's *Saving Jessica Lynch*, despite Lynch's lack of memory and the fact that some circumstances of the rescue have been questioned by the media and Lynch herself.

CHAPTER 8

The Bias of Language, the Bias of Pictures

WHEN A TELEVISION NEWS show distorts the truth by altering or manufacturing facts (through re-creations), the television viewer is defenseless even if a re-creation is properly labeled. Viewers are still vulnerable to misinformation since they will not know (at least in the case of docudramas) what parts are fiction and what parts are not. But the problems of verisimilitude posed by re-creations pale to insignificance when compared to the problems viewers face when encountering a straight (no-monkey-business) show. All news shows, in a sense, are re-creations in that what we hear and see on them are attempts to represent actual events and are not the events themselves. Perhaps, to avoid ambiguity, we might call all news shows "re-presentations" instead of re-creations. These re-presentations come to us in two forms: language and pictures. The question then arises: what do viewers have to know about language and pictures in order to be properly armed to defend themselves against the seductions of eloquence (to use Bertrand Russell's apt phrase)?

Let us take language first. Below are three principles that, in our opinion, are an essential part of the analytical equipment a viewer must bring to any encounter with a news show.

1. Whatever anyone says something is, it isn't.

This sounds more complex—and maybe more pretentious—than it actually is. What it means is that there is a difference between the world of events and the world of words about events. The job of an honest reporter is to find words, and the appropriate tone in presenting them, that will come as close to evoking the event as possible. But since no two people will use exactly the same words to describe an event, we must acknowledge that for every verbal description of an event, there are multiple possible alternatives. You may demonstrate this to your own satisfaction by writing a two-paragraph description of a dinner you had with at least two other people, then asking the others who were present if each of them would also write, independently, a two-paragraph description of the same dinner. We should be very surprised if all of the descriptions include the same words, in the same order, emphasize the same things, and express the same feelings. In other words, "the dinner itself" is largely a nonverbal event. The words people use to describe this event are not the event itself and are only abstracted re-presentations of the event. What does this mean for a television viewer? It means that the viewer must never assume that the words spoken on a television news show represent exactly what happened. Since there are so many alternative ways of describing what happened, the viewer must be on guard against assuming that he or she has heard "the absolute truth."

2. Language operates at various levels of abstraction.

This means that there is a level of language whose purpose is to *describe* an event. There is also a level of language whose purpose is to *evaluate* an event. Even more, there is a level of language whose purpose is to *infer* what is unknown on the basis of what is known. The usual way to make these distinctions clear is through sentences such as the following three:

Manny Freebus is five foot eight and weighs 235 pounds.
Manny Freebus is grossly fat.
Manny Freebus eats too much.

The first sentence may be said to be language as pure description. It involves no judgments and no inferences. The second sentence is a description of sorts, but is mainly a judgment that the speaker makes of the "event" known as Manny Freebus. The third sentence is an inference based on observations the speaker has made. It fact, a statement about the unknown based on the known. As it happens, we know Manny Freebus and can tell you that he eats no more than the average person but suffers from a glandular condition that keeps him overweight. Therefore, anyone who concluded from observing Manny's shape that he eats too much has made a false inference. A good guess, but false nonetheless.

You can watch television news programs from now until doomsday and never come across any statement about Manny Freebus. But you will constantly come across the three kinds of statements we have been discussing: descriptions, judgments, and inferences. And it is important for a viewer to distinguish among them. For example, you might hear an anchor introduce a story by saying: "Today Congress ordered an investigation of the explosive issue of whether Ronald Reagan's presidential campaign made a deal with Iran in 1980 to delay the release of American hostages until after the election." This statement is, of course, largely descriptive, but includes the judgmental word "explosive" as part of the report. We need hardly point out that what is explosive to one person may seem trivial to another. We do not say that the news writer has no business to include his or her judgment of this investigation. We do say that the viewer has to be aware that a judgment has been made. In fact, even the phrase "made a deal" (why not "arranged with Iran"?) has a somewhat sleazy connotation that implies a judgment of sorts. If, in the same news report, we are told that the evidence for such a secret deal is weak and that "only an investigation with subpoena power can establish the truth," we must know that we have left the arena of factual language and have moved into the land of inference. An investigation with subpoena power may be a good idea, but whether it can establish the truth is a guess on the journalist's part, and a viewer ought to know that.

3. Almost all words have connotative meanings.

This suggests that even when attempting to use purely descriptive language, a journalist cannot avoid expressing an attitude about what he or she is saying. For example, here is the opening sentence of an anchor's report about national examinations: "For the first time in the nation's history, high-level education policymakers have designed the elements for a national examination system similar to the one advocated by President Bush." This sentence certainly looks like it is pure description, although it is filled with ambiguities. Is this the first time in our history that this has been done? Or only the first time that high-level education policymakers have done it? Or is it the first time something has been designed that is similar to what the president has advocated? But let us put those questions aside. (After all, there are limits to how analytical one ought to be.) Instead, we might concentrate on such words as "high-level," "policymakers," and "designed." Speaking for ourselves, we are by no means sure that we know what a "high-level policymaker" is, although it sounds awfully impressive. It is certainly better than a low-level policymaker, although how one would distinguish between the two is a bit of a mystery. Come to think of it, a low-level policymaker must be pretty good, too, since anyone who makes policy must be important. It comes as no surprise, therefore, that what was done was "designed." To design something usually implies careful thought, preparation, organization, and coherence. People design buildings, bridges, and furniture. If your experience has been anything like ours, you will know that reports are almost never designed; they are usually "thrown together," and it is quite a compliment to say that a report was designed. The journalist who paid this compliment was certainly entitled to do it, even though he may not have been aware of what he was doing. He probably thought he had made a simple description, avoiding any words that would imply favor or disfavor. But if so, he was defeated in his effort because language tends to be emotion laden. Because it is people who do the talking, the talk almost always includes a feeling, an attitude, a judgment. In a sense, every language contains the history of a people's feelings about the world. Our words are baskets of emotion. Smart journalists, of course, know this. And so do smart audiences. Smart audiences don't blame anyone for this state of affairs. They are, however, prepared for it.

It is not our intention to provide a minicourse in semantics. Even if we could, we are well aware that no viewer could apply analytic principles all the time or even much of the time. Anchors and reporters talk too fast and too continuously for any of us to monitor most of their sentences. Besides, who would want to do that for most of the stories on a news show? If you have a sense of what is important, you will probably judge most news stories to be fluff or nonsense or irrelevancies not worthy of your analytic weaponry. But there are times when stories appear that are of major significance from your point of view. These are the times when your level of attention will reach a peak and you must call upon your best powers of interpretation. In those moments, you need to draw on whatever you know about the relationship between language and reality; about the distinctions among statements of fact, judgment, and inference; about the connotative meanings of words. When this is done properly, viewers are no longer passive consumers of news but active participants in a kind of dialogue between a news show and themselves. A viewer may even find that he or she is "talking back to the television set" (which is the title of a book by former FCC commissioner Nicholas Johnson). In our view, nothing could be healthier for the sanity and well-being of our nation than to have 100 million viewers talking back to their television news shows every night and twice on Sunday.

Now we must turn to the problem of pictures. It is often said that a picture is worth a thousand words. One could also say that the *lack* of a picture—a censored image—is worth a thousand words (e.g., censorship of pictures of coffins of Americans killed in Iraq). And it is probably equally true that one word is worth a thousand pictures, at least sometimes—like when it comes to understanding the world we live in. Indeed, the whole problem with news on television comes down to this: all the words uttered in an hour of news coverage could be printed on one page of a newspaper. And the world cannot be understood in one page. Of course, there is a compensation: television offers pictures, and the pictures move. Moving pictures are a kind of language in themselves, but the language of pictures differs radically from oral and written language, and the differences are crucial for understanding television news.

To begin with, pictures, especially single pictures, speak only in particularities. Their vocabulary is limited to concrete representation. Unlike words and sentences, a picture does not present to us an idea or concept about the world, except as we use language itself to convert the image to idea. By itself, a picture cannot deal with the unseen, the remote, the internal, the abstract. It does not speak of "man," only of *a* man; not of "tree," only of *a* tree. You cannot produce an image of "nature," any more than an image of "the sea." You can only show a particular fragment of the here and now: a cliff in a given terrain, in a certain condition of light; a wave at a moment in time, from a particular point of view. And just as nature and the sea cannot be photographed, such larger abstractions as truth, honor, love, and falsehood cannot be talked about in the lexicon of individual pictures. For *showing* and *talking about* are two very different kinds of processes: individual pictures give us the world as object; language, the world as idea. There is no such thing in nature as "man" or "tree." The universe offers no such categories or simplifications, only flux and infinite variety. The picture documents and celebrates the particularities of the universe's infinite variety. Language makes them comprehensible.

Of course, moving pictures, video with sound, may bridge the gap by juxtaposing images, symbols, sound, and music. Such images can present emotions and rudimentary ideas. They can suggest the panorama of nature and the joys and miseries of humankind.

Picture: smoke pouring from a window; cut to people coughing, an ambulance racing to a hospital, a tombstone in a cemetery.

Picture: jet planes firing rockets, explosions, lines of foreign soldiers surrendering, the American flag waving in the wind.

Nonetheless, keep in mind that when terrorists want to prove to the world that their kidnap victims are still alive, they photograph them holding a copy of a recent newspaper. The dateline on the newspaper provides the proof that the photograph was taken on or after that date. Without the help of the written word, film and videotape cannot portray temporal dimensions with any precision. Consider a film clip showing an aircraft carrier at sea. One might be able to identify the ship as Russian or American, but there would be little or no way of telling where in the world the carrier was, where it was headed, or when the pictures were taken. It is only through language—words spoken over the pictures or reproduced in them—that the image of the aircraft carrier takes on specific meaning.

Still, it is possible to enjoy the image of the carrier for its own sake. One might find the hugeness of the vessel interesting; it signifies military power on the move. There is a certain drama in watching the planes come in at high speeds and skid to a stop on the deck. Suppose the ship were burning: that would be even more interesting. This leads to an important point about the language of pictures. Moving pictures favor images that change. That is why violence and dynamic destruction find their way on to television so often. When something is destroyed violently, it is altered in a highly visible way; hence the entrancing power of fire. Fire gives visual form to the ideas of consumption, disappearance, death: the thing that burned is actually taken away by fire. It is at this very basic level that fires make a good subject for television news.

Something was here, now it's gone, and the change is recorded on film.

Earthquakes and typhoons have the same power. Before the viewer's eyes the world is taken apart. If a television viewer has relatives in Mexico City and an earthquake occurs there, then he or she may take a special interest in the images of destruction as a report from a specific place and time; that is, one may look at television pictures for information about an important event. But film of an earthquake can be interesting even if the viewer cares nothing about the event itself. Which is only to say, as we noted earlier, that there is another way of participating in the news: as a spectator who desires to be entertained. To see buildings topple is exciting, no matter where the buildings are. The world turns to dust before our eyes.

Those who produce television news in America know that their medium favors images that move. That is why they are wary of talking heads, people who simply appear in front of a camera and speak. When talking heads appear on television, there is nothing to record or document, no change in process. In the cinema, the situation is somewhat different. On a movie screen, close-ups of a good actor speaking dramatically can sometimes be interesting to watch. When Clint Eastwood narrows his eyes and challenges his rival to shoot first, the spectator sees the cool rage of the Eastwood character take form, and the narrowing of the eyes is dramatic. But much of the effect of this small movement depends on the size of the movie screen and the darkness of the theater, which make Eastwood and his every action "larger than life."

The television screen is smaller than life (though growing). It occupies about 15 percent of the viewer's visual field (compared to about 70 percent for the movie screen). It is not set in a darkened theater closed off from the world but in the viewer's ordinary living space. This means that visual changes must be more extreme and more dramatic to be interesting on television. A narrowing of the eyes will not do. A car crash, an earthquake, a burning factory are better.

With these principles in mind, let us examine more closely the structure of a typical newscast, and we will include in the discussion not only the pictures but the nonlinguistic symbols that make up a television show. For example, in America almost all news shows begin with music, the tone of which suggests important events about to unfold. The music is crucial, for it equates the news with various forms of drama and ritual—the opera, for example, or a wedding procession—in which musical themes underscore the meaning of the event. Music takes us immediately into the realm of the symbolic, a world that is not to be taken literally. After all, when events unfold in the real world, they do so without musical accompaniment. More symbolism follows. The sound of Teletype machines can sometimes be heard in the studio, not because it is impossible to screen this noise out, but because the sound is a kind of music in itself. It tells us that data is pouring in from all corners of the globe, a sensation reinforced by the world map in the background (or clocks noting the time on different continents). The fact is that Teletype machines are never used in TV news rooms, having been replaced by silent computer terminals. When heard, they have only a symbolic function.

The set itself is filled with symbols, from the massive authoritarian desks the anchors sit at to the pens the anchors hold, the costumes provided by Ralph Lauren and Ann Taylor, the colors of the backdrop, the shapes of the furniture, and so on.

Already, then, before a single news item is introduced, a great deal has been communicated. We know that we are in the presence of a symbolic event, a form of theater in which the day's events are to be dramatized. This theater takes the entire globe as its subject, although it may look at the world from the perspective of a single nation. A certain tension is present, like the atmosphere in a theater just before the curtain goes up. The tension is represented by the music, perhaps the staccato beat of the Teletype machines, and often the sight of news workers scurrying around, typing reports, and answering phones. As a technical matter, it would be no problem to build a set in which the newsroom staff remained off camera, invisible to the viewer, but an important theatrical effect would be lost. By being busy on camera, the workers help communicate urgency about the events at hand, which suggests that situations are changing so rapidly that constant revision of the news is necessary.

The staff in the background also helps signal the importance of the person in the center, the anchor, "in command" of both the staff and the news. The anchor plays the role of host. He or she welcomes us to the newscast and welcomes us back from the different locations we visit during the filmed reports.

Many features of the newscast help the anchor to establish the impression of control. These are usually equated with production values in broadcasting. They include such things as graphics that tell the viewer what is being shown, or maps and charts that suddenly appear on the screen and disappear on cue, or the orderly procession from story to story. They also include the absence of gaps, or dead time, during the broadcast, even the simple fact that the news starts and ends at a certain hour. These common features are thought of as purely technical matters, which a professional crew handles as matter of course. But they are also symbols of a dominant theme of television news: the imposition of an orderly world called "the news" upon the disorderly flow of events. At the conclusion of some newscasts the anchor is seen writing, perhaps signing her name, on the news script, signing off on the events of the day.

While the form of a news broadcast emphasizes tidiness and control, its content can best be described as fragmented.

Because time is so precious on television, because the nature of the medium favors dynamic visual images, and because the pressures of a commercial structure require the news to hold its audience above all else, there is rarely any attempt to explain issues in depth or place events in their proper context. The news moves nervously from a warehouse fire to a court decision, from a guerrilla war to a World Cup match, the quality of the footage most often determining the length of the story. Certain stories show up only because they offer dramatic pictures. Bleachers collapse in South America: hundreds of people are crushed—a perfect television news story, for the cameras can record the face of disaster in all its anguish. Back in Washington, a new budget is approved by Congress. There is nothing to photograph because a budget is not a physical event; it is a document full of language and numbers. So the producers of the news will show a photo of the document itself, focusing on the cover where it says "Budget of the United States of America." Or maybe they will send a camera crew to the government printing plant where copies of the budget are produced. That evening, while the contents of the budget are summarized by a voice-over, the viewer will see stacks of documents being loaded into boxes at the government printing plant. Then a few of the budget's more important provisions will be flashed on the screen in written form, but this is such a time-consuming process—using television as a printed page—that the producers keep it to a minimum. In short, the budget is not "televisable," and for that reason its time on the news must be brief. The bleacher collapse will get more time that evening.

While appearing somewhat chaotic, these disparate stories are not just dropped in the news program helter-skelter. The appearance of a scattershot story order is really orchestrated to draw the audience from one story to the next—from one section to the next—through the commercial breaks to the end of the show. The story order is constructed to hold and build the viewership rather than place events in context or explain issues in depth.

Of course, it is a tendency of journalism in general to concentrate on the surface of events rather than underlying conditions; this is as true for the newspaper as is for the newscast. But several features of television undermine whatever efforts journalists may make to give sense to the world. One is that a television broadcast is a series of events that occur in sequence, and the sequence is the same for all viewers. This is not true for a newspaper page, which displays many items simultaneously, allowing readers to choose the order in which they read them. If newspaper readers want only a summary of the latest tax bill, they can read the headline and the first paragraph of an article, and if they want more, they can keep reading. In a sense, then, everyone reads a different newspaper, for no two readers will read (or ignore) the same items.

But all television viewers see the same broadcast. They have no choices. A report is either in the broadcast or out, which means that anything of narrow interest is unlikely to be included. As the late NBC News executive Reuven Frank once explained:

> A newspaper, for example, can easily afford to print an item of conceivable interest to only a fraction of its readers. A television news program must be put together with the assumption that each item will be of some interest to everyone that watches. Every time a newspaper includes a feature which will attract a specialized group it can assume it is adding at least a little bit to its circulation. To the degree a television news program includes an item of this sort . . . it must assume that its audience will diminish.

The need to include "everyone," an identifying feature of commercial television in all its forms, prevents journalists from offering lengthy or complex explanations, or from tracing the sequence of events leading up to today's headlines. One of the ironies of political life in modern democracies is that many problems that concern the "general welfare" are of interest only to specialized groups. Arms control, for example, is an issue that literally concerns everyone in the world, and yet the language of arms control and the complexity of the subject are so daunting that only a minority of people can actually follow the issue from week to week and month to month. If it wants to act responsibly, a newspaper can at least make available more information about arms control than most people want. Commercial television cannot afford to do so.

But even if commercial television could afford to do so, it wouldn't. The fact that television news is principally made up of moving pictures prevents it from offering lengthy, coherent explanations of events. A television news show reveals the world as a series of unrelated, fragmentary moments. It does not, and cannot be expected to, offer a sense of coherence or meaning. What does this suggest to a TV viewer? That the viewer must come with a prepared mind: information, opinions, a sense of proportion, an articulate value system. To the viewer lacking such mental equipment, a news program is only a kind of rousing light show. Here a falling building, there a five-alarm fire, everywhere the world as an object, much without meaning, connections, or continuity. Edward R. Murrow put it this way: "This instrument can teach, it can illuminate; yes, and it can even inspire. But it can do so only to the extent that humans are determined to use it to those ends. Otherwise it is merely wires and lights in a box."

CHAPTER 9

The Commercial

THE BACKBONE, THE HEART, the soul, the fuel, the DNA (choose whatever metaphor you wish) of nonpublic television in America is the commercial. This is as true of the television news show as it is any other form of programming. To have a realistic understanding of TV news you must consider two dimensions of the commercial. The first concerns money; the second, social values.

Let's talk business first, which means we must begin with the magic initials CPM. CPM is what makes the cash registers sing for news and other programs. It stands for "cost per thousand" (Roman numeral M = thousand). Specifically, it is the cost to an advertiser for each thousand people reached by a commercial. When we last checked, the CPM for the evening newscasts was approximately $6.50 to $7.00 per thirty-second spot, for the broad household audience. That means an advertiser must spend at least $6.50 to reach each thousand people watching the evening weekday news. That works out to a bit more than half a cent for each viewer delivered, as counted by the rating services. The network, in effect, promises to deliver the audience but doesn't promise that any of them will watch the commercials or buy the products. If you use your TiVo to fast-forward through the spots or step out of the room during the commercial to make a salami sandwich, the advertiser still gets charged. But with audiences in the millions, enough people see the commercials and buy enough products to make the system work.

Naturally, programs with high ratings (even if they have a correspondingly high CPM) are attractive to advertisers because they want to reach as many potential customers as possible at one time. News programs fill the bill. On any given weekday evening, around 25 million people are watching the network news, with 60 million more watching local news in the early evening and late night. About 12.5 million people watch morning news programs. For an advertiser who wants to reach a large audience, network news easily surpasses other news media; e.g., newspapers and magazines. *USA Today* boasts the largest daily paper circulation, a little more than 2.5 million. *The Wall Street Journal* is next with 2 million. *Time* magazine has a weekly circulation of 4.1 million people. The Sunday morning news shows *Face the Nation, Meet the Press,* and *This Week* deliver a combined audience of 9 million viewers. *The NewsHour with Jim Lehrer* delivers about 2.4 million viewers each night. Compare all that with the more than 25 million people tuned to the ABC, CBS, and NBC news every weekday evening.

But audience size is by no means the only factor advertisers are interested in. Even more important are demographics. Each news program has a demographic profile; that is, a statistical picture of the age, sex, and income of those who habitually watch the program. Advertisers of skateboards will tend to advertise on news programs with young viewers; advertisers of arthritis medicine will place their commercials on news programs with an "older demographic."

It sounds simple enough but it isn't. Advertising agency spot buyers may have a difficult time trying to figure out where to spend the advertiser's dollar because a show with a small audience can make its news program a good "buy" by lowering its CPM, and a show with the demographics that match the advertiser's target audience may be worth a premium. The time of year will further affect the price (the first and third quarters of the year are less expensive). So news programs try to increase their ratings and attract the coveted demographic. For example, during the week of December 18, 2006, *NBC Nightly News with Brian Williams* was the number-one network news program in the desirable twenty-five- to fifty-four-year-old demo, with a 2.4 rating (each rating point represents 1 percent of the 112.8 million households in the United States). But an advertiser shopping for a bargain might decide to buy the *CBS Evening News with Katie Couric*, with a 1.9 rating in the twenty-five- to fifty-four-year-old demographic, or ABC's *World News with Charles Gibson*, with a 2.2. In that same demographic, NBC delivered 2.888 million people, ABC 2.733 million, and CBS 2.349 million.

Beside sheer numbers of viewers, ratings also purport to tell what percentage of all viewers are watching any given show. Ratings numbers are usually quoted in pairs, such as *NBC Nightly News* total homes delivered: 6.4/13. That means 6.4 percent of the total TV-watching households in the country had the show tuned in and 13 percent of all the households with a TV turned on at that precise moment were watching that show.

After those numbers have been carefully analyzed, spot buyers look at rate cards (which list the price of each news show's commercials) and make their decisions with the help of computers. On NBC News, a thirty-second spot might cost about $60,000. With about eight minutes of commercial time available each night, a network news show can generate about $480,000 a night, or $2.4 million each week. Journalism.org quotes TNS Media Intelligence as estimating that in 2005 NBC's evening news earned $159 million, CBS earned about $162 million, and ABC earned about $168 million, even though NBC had higher overall ratings. The reason given was that much of network advertising is bundled across more than one program or platform, such as NBC network and MSNBC. Moreover, because of the appeal of news programs, commercials placed adjacent to a news show will bring a premium price, as will commercials that lead in to local news programs. Where once there was one hour of news, local and network, many markets now feature two- and three-hour news programs. As we write, a countertrend is under way: reducing evening news program time in favor of double access; that is, one hour of syndicated news preceding and following prime time. Syndicated shows such as *Access Hollywood*, *Wheel of Fortune*, *Entertainment Tonight*, *Oprah*, *Judge Judy*, and *Primer Impacto* (Spanish language) have replaced many locally produced news programs.

What all of this means is that the stakes in the ad game are astronomical. PricewaterhouseCoopers estimated that the global TV network market in 2003 was $130.7 billion. It also estimated that U.S. broadcast and cable TV networks made $47 billion in 2003 and $52.3 billion in 2004.

It is estimated that NBC, ABC, CBS, and Fox take in at least $4.5 billion a year in prime-time sales. Each rating point is worth about $10,000 for each thirty-second network commercial, but a commercial on a hit series can bring in $32,000 more per commercial than what is charged on an average series. That adds up to $224,000 more per week. Don Hewitt, former producer of the extremely successful *60 Minutes* news program, has boasted that his show makes $70 million a year in profit for CBS (although industry figures estimate that the show earns only $40 million a year). According to 2004 TNS data, annual ad revenue for NBC's ubiquitous *Dateline* franchise was $232.3 million. CBS's *60 Minutes* made $108 million, *60 Minutes II*'s ad revenue was $62 million, and *20/20* took in $77 million. CBS's *48 Hours Mystery*, which premiered as *48 Hours*, had ad revenue of $78 million in 2005. In 2004, *Nightline* took in $75 million. It has since changed its host and adjusted its format to appeal to a younger audience.

With so much money being spent just for airtime, advertisers and their agencies want their messages to be effective. To make sure that happens, they bring in a small army of specialists, people who are experts in making commercials. Over months of work, artists, statisticians, writers, psychologists, researchers, musicians, cinematographers, lighting consultants, camera operators, producers, directors, set builders, composers, models, actors, audio experts, executives, and technicians will toil for one single objective: to make a commercial that will make you buy a product or idea. Time and talent costs can be $500,000 for a short commercial.

There are approximately twenty-five thousand different commercials on network television every year. This is necessary, in part, to keep pace with the two hundred or so new items that appear every week on drugstore and supermarket shelves across the country. This means that advertisers have to produce commercials that will be noticed and will motivate viewers to spend money. The competition is fierce and continuous. At the same time, the costs for advertisers have gotten so high that the sixty-second commercial, once the backbone of broadcast TV, has given way to the shorter thirty-second spot, which is often broken down into ten- and fifteen-second commercials. This "piggybacking" does bring down the cost of each commercial (a fifteen-second commercial will cost about

20 percent less than a thirty-second spot), but it also squeezes four or more commercials into the same time slot that one commercial used to fill. What this means is that next year, if you watch TV as much as the average American, you will be exposed to something on the order of over thirty-nine thousand minutes of commercials.

That number will include commercials that are part of "line campaigns." These are commercials featuring a whole line of products made by one company. For example, Colgate-Palmolive has made commercials that sold Colgate Junior toothpaste, regular Colgate toothpaste, Colgate anticavity mouth rinse, Colgate tartar-control toothpaste, and two kinds of Colgate toothbrushes—all that in one sixty-second commercial. Companies favor the idea of multipurpose spots because they can sell several products for the cost of one commercial. Corporations also believe that the name of their company is as important a selling point as the names individual products. But it also means more ad clutter for the average viewer, and we are not even considering the promotional spots cajoling you to stay tuned or watch other shows.

In an experimental ad campaign, Phillips Electronics became the sole sponsor for one night's edition of *NBC Nightly News* in December 2006. Instead of the normal seven minutes, Phillips used just over sixty seconds of ad time to emphasize its theme of "sense and simplicity." That freed up an extra six minutes of airtime for news, which resulted in several additional stories. Anchor Brian Williams says the response was highly favorable, with higher ratings and some viewers pledging to buy Phillips's products. ABC's *World News with Charles Gibson* had a single sponsor for each Monday newscast in April 2007. ABC said it would add five minutes to each newscast, during which it would accommodate a series of reports on serious issues around the world.

There is much more that can be said about the economics of commercials, but what we *have* said, we believe, are the basics of the business. It is all about serious money. But commercials are also about the serious manipulation of our social and psychic lives. There are, in fact, some critics who say that commercials are a new, albeit degraded, means of religious expression in that most of them take the form of parables, teaching people what the good life consists of. It is a claim not to be easily dismissed. Let us take as an example an imaginary commercial for a mouthwash, but one that replicates a common pattern. We'll call the product Fresh Taste. The commercial will run for thirty seconds, and, like any decent parable, will have a beginning, a middle, and an end. The beginning will show a man and woman saying good-bye, at her door, after an evening out. The woman tilts her head, expecting to be kissed. The man steps back, in a state of polite revulsion, and says, "Well, Barbara, it was nice meeting you. I'll call sometime soon." Barbara is disappointed. And so ends act 1, which is accomplished in ten seconds. Act 2 shows Barbara talking to her roommate. "This always happens to me, Joan," she laments. "What's wrong with me?" Joan is ready. "Your problem," she says, "is your mouthwash. Yours is too mediciny and doesn't protect you long enough. You should try Fresh Taste." Joan holds up a new bottle, which Barbara examines with an optimistic gleam in her eye. That's act 2. Also ten seconds. Act 3, the final ten, shows Barbara and the once-reluctant young man getting off a plane in Hawaii. Both are in the early stages of ecstasy, and we are to understand that they are on their honeymoon. Fresh Taste has done it again.

Let's consider exactly what it *has* done. To begin with, the structure of the commercial is as compact and well organized as the parable of the prodigal son, maybe even better organized and certainly more compressed. The first ten seconds show the problem: Barbara has trouble with her social life but is unaware of the cause. The second ten seconds show the solution: Barbara has bad breath, which could be remedied by her buying a different product. The last ten seconds show the moral of the story: if you know the right product to buy, you will find happiness.

Imagine, now, a slight alteration in the commercial. The first ten seconds remain the same. The change comes in act 2. Barbara wonders what's wrong with her but gets a somewhat different answer from Joan. "'What's wrong with you?" Joan asks. "I'll tell you what's wrong with you. You are boring. You are dull, dull, dull. You haven't read a book in four years. You don't know the difference between Mozart and Bruce Springsteen. You couldn't even name the *continent* that Nigeria is on. It's a wonder that any man would want to spend more than ten minutes with you!" A chastened Barbara replies, "You are right. But what can I do?" "What can you do?" Joan answers. "I'll tell you what you can do. Start by taking a course or two at a local university. Join a book club. Get some tickets to the opera. Read the *New York Times* once in a while." "But that will take forever, months, maybe years," says Barbara. "That's right," replies Joan, "so you'd better start now." The commercial ends with Joan handing Barbara a copy of Freud's *Civilization and Its Discontents*. Barbara looks forlorn but begins to finger the pages.

This, too, is a parable, but its lesson is so different from that of the first commercial that there is no chance you will ever see anything like it on television. Its point is that there are no simple or fast solutions to life's important problems; specifically, there is no chemical that can make you desirable: attractiveness must come from within. This idea, which is a commonplace in the Judeo-Christian tradition, is the exact opposite of what almost all commercials teach.

As we said, the average American TV viewer will see over thirty-nine thousand minutes of commercials next year. Some of them will be quite straightforward, and some funny; some will be spoofs of other commercials, and some mysterious and exotic. But many of them will have the structure of our hypothetical commercial and will urge the following ideas: whatever problem you face (lack of self-esteem, lack of good taste, lack of attractiveness, lack of social acceptance), it can be solved, solved fast, and solved through a drug, a detergent, a machine, or a salable technique. You are, in fact, helpless unless you know about the product that can remake you and set you on the road to paradise. You must, in short, become a born-again consumer, redeem yourself, and find peace.

There are even commercials that show us a vision of hell should we fail to buy the right product. We are thinking, for example, of the 2007 State Farm Auto Insurance commercial, which takes its symbolism straight from Dante's *Inferno*. Some poor guy comes out of a grocery store and finds that the name Brad is scratched on his car door in big letters. He calls his insurance company, and an irritating phone operator explains to him that his low-rate policy only covers scratches of full names. She explains that he'd be covered if Bradley, Bradford, or Brady were scratched on the car but not nicknames. Presumably, the poor guy must drive around forever in perdition with "Brad" etched on his car door, all because he bought his auto policy from the wrong company.

An earlier version of this "wrong product" commercial was the numerous American Express traveler's check spots that showed, for example, a typical American couple checking out of a hotel in some strange city, perhaps Istanbul. The husband reaches for his wallet but cannot find it. He has lost it, along with his traveler's checks. The check-out clerk asks, with hope in his eyes, if the lost checks were American Express traveler's checks, for if they were, they are easily enough replaced. The husband, his voice practically gone, says they were not. The clerk shrugs his shoulders, as if to say, "Then, there is no hope for you." Perhaps you have seen this commercial. Have you ever wondered what happens to these people? Do they wander forever in limbo? Will they always be in an alien land far from home? Will they ever see their children again? Is this not a just punishment for their ignorance, for their lack of attention? The truth, after all, was available to them. Why were they not able to see it?

Perhaps you are thinking we exaggerate. After all, most people don't pay all that much attention to commercials. But that, in fact, is one of the reasons commercials are so effective. People do not usually analyze them. Neither, we might say, do people analyze biblical parables, which are often ambiguous; some, as in the case of the parable of the prodigal son, seem even downright unfair. Like biblical parables, commercial messages invade our consciousness, seep into our souls. Even if you are half-awake when commercials run, thirty thousand of them will begin to penetrate your indifference. In the end, it is hard not to believe.

Whether you call the structure and messages of commercials "religious," "quasi-religious," "antireligious," or something else, it is clear that they are the most constant and voluminous source of value propaganda in our culture. Commercials are almost never about anything trivial. Mouthwash commercials are not about bad breath. They are about the need for social acceptance and, frequently, about the need to be sexually attractive. Beer commercials are almost always about a man's need to share the values of a peer group. An automobile commercial is usually about the need for autonomy or social status, a deodorant commercial about one's fear of nature. Television commercials are about products only in the sense that the story of Jonah is about the anatomy of whales, which is to say, they aren't. Like the story of Jonah, they set out to teach us lessons about the solutions to life's problems, and that is why we are inclined to think of them as a corrupt modality of spiritual instruction.

Boredom, anxiety, rejection, fear, envy, sloth—in TV commercials there are remedies for each of these, and more. The remedies are called Scope, Comet, Toyota, Bufferin, Alka-Seltzer, and Budweiser. They take the place of good works, restraint, piety, awe, humility, and transcendence. On TV commercials, moral deficiencies as we customarily think of them do not really exist. A commercial for Alka-Seltzer, for example, does not teach you to avoid overeating. Gluttony is perfectly acceptable—maybe even desirable. The point of the commercial is that your gluttony is no problem. Alka-Seltzer will handle it. The seven deadly sins, in other words, are problems to be solved through chemistry and technology. On commercials, there are no intimations of the conventional roads to spiritual redemption. But there is original sin, and it consists of our having been ignorant of a product that offers happiness. We may achieve a state of grace by attending to the good news about it, which will appear every six or seven minutes. It follows from this that he or she is most devout who knows of the largest array of products; they are heretics who willfully ignore what is there to be used.

Part of the reason commercials are effective is that they are, in a sense, invisible. When you check the TV listings in your local newspaper or *TV Guide*, do you find the commercials listed? Since there will be more than eleven minutes of commercials, teases, and promotional announcements in a thirty-minute news show, would it not be relevant to indicate what the content of 36 percent of the show will be? But, of course, the commercials will not be listed. They are simply taken for granted, which is why so few people regard it as strange that a commercial should proceed a news story about an earthquake in Chile or, even worse, follow a news story about an earthquake in Chile. It is difficult to measure the effect on an audience that has been shown pictures of an earthquake's devastation and immediately afterward is subjected to commercials for Crest toothpaste, Scope, United Airlines, and Alka-Seltzer. Our best guess is that the earthquake takes on a surrealistic aspect; it is certainly trivialized. It is as if the program's producer is saying, "You needn't grieve or worry about what you are seeing. In a minute or so, we will make you happy with some good news about how to make your teeth whiter."

Of course, an argument may be made that a concern over how to make your teeth whiter is far more important than your lamentations about an earthquake; that is to say, advertising fuels a capitalist economy. For a market economy to work, the population must be made to believe that it is in need of continuous improvement. If you are quite satisfied with your teeth, your hair, your 2003 Honda, and your weight, you will not be an avid consumer. You will be especially worthless to the economy if your mind is preoccupied with worldly events. If you are not an avid consumer, the engine of the economy slows and then stalls. Therefore, the thematic thrust of advertising is to take your mind off earthquakes, the homeless, and other irrelevancies and to get you to think about your inadequate self and how you can get better. Of course, the traditional point of journalism is to turn you away from yourself and toward the world. Thus in the intermingling of news and commercials we have a struggle of sorts between two different orientations. Each tries to refute the other. It would be interesting to know which point of view will triumph in the long run.

CHAPTER 10

Television in the Courtroom

WE WOULD NOT BE surprised if many Americans believe that if something is not on a television news show it isn't news—or at least not important news. Some may also believe that anything and everything *ought* to be on television. Many television journalists come close to believing that, and they usually defend their view by mumbling something about "the public's right to know." How much the "public" has a right to know, and when and why and how, are, in fact, troubling questions. Does the "public" have a right, for example, to see and hear what goes on in a confessional? Of course not, most will say. That is strictly a private matter between a priest and a sinner. Well, then, does the "public" have a right to see and hear what goes on in a public school classroom, which, after all, is supported by tax dollars? Some would say yes, provided that the visitor's presence does not interfere with the lesson. But everyone can't get into a classroom. How about televising the lesson so that everyone has access to what's going on there? And what if the teacher objects? Or the students? Should they be permitted to bar a television camera from coming into their classroom? Some would say yes: what happens between teacher and students is at least a quasi-private matter, and the "public" ought not to be forced upon them. Some would say no: The "public" pays for the school, the teachers, and everything else related to the enterprise. If it wants cameras there, cameras should be there—whether or not teachers and students object. It is a tricky issue but somewhat irrelevant since almost nobody is *that* interested in classrooms, least of all television journalists.

But as for courtrooms, that is a different matter. Many people are fascinated by courtrooms, as evidenced by the success of representations from *Perry Mason* to *Judge Judy* to *Boston Legal*. Television news directors and producers are well aware of this fascination, and most universally favor the idea of televising actual trials. Televised trials make for good television, which means large audiences, which means higher rates for commercials, which probably means better salary deals when contracts are negotiated. Besides, many television journalists say, the "public" has a right to know.

We have put the word "public" in quotation marks because it has a somewhat ambiguous meaning, especially in the context of the dispute about the appropriateness of televising courtroom trials. There are, in fact, two meanings to the word "public" that are quite different from each other. The first meaning is, simply, the opposite of secret or private. In America and other civilized countries, trials are always public in that journalists, interested parties, and ordinary citizens have access to the proceedings. There is nothing secret about the matter except in those instances where a judge confers "privately" with opposing counsels on some technical legal issue. The other meaning of "public" refers to a huge, undifferentiated audience: the proverbial man and woman in the street who may or may not have an interest in what journalists believe it is their right to know. Everyone, we assume, is in favor of keeping trials public (in the sense of the first meaning). But not everyone agrees that the public (in its second meaning) has a right to see trials on television.

In 2005, Court TV lost its bid to reverse New York State's fifty-three-year-old ban on cameras in the courtroom. In a seven-to-zero decision, the court of appeals ruled that no constitutional rights are being violated by keeping television cameras out of the courtroom and said it is the legislature's job to decide whether trials may be televised. In *Courtroom Television Network v. State of New York*, Judge George Bundy Smith wrote, "We agree with the Supreme Court and the Appellate Division that there is no First Amendment or article I, section 8 right to televise a trial. . . . The record also is consistent with New York's statutory scheme which guarantees public trials, but primacy to fair trial rights."

Additionally, the court made clear that the press has no greater right of access to the courtroom than the general public. But the court ruled that New York State's law does not prevent the press, including television journalists, from attending trials and reporting on the proceedings. What the news media cannot do under the statute is bring cameras into the courtroom. Judge Smith wrote, "This is not a restriction on the openness of court proceedings but rather on what means can be used in order to gather news. The media's access is thus guaranteed. But it does not extend to a right to televise those proceedings."

In other court decisions, there were a number of concerns about the presence of cameras at the trial, including the prejudicial impact of pretrial publicity on the jurors, the impact on the truthfulness of the witnesses, responsibilities placed on the trial judge to assure a fair trial, and the impact on the defendant. In one case, the U.S. Supreme Court wrote, "A defendant on trial for a specific crime is entitled to his day in court, not in a stadium, or a city or nationwide arena."

To get to the heart of the matter, we must provide a short history of the controversy, which began with the invention and development of photography in the mid-nineteenth century. At that point, it became possible to provide citizens with a view of the American court system never before witnessed except by the tiny minority that had actually been in courts. But from the outset, there were concerns expressed that the presence of still cameras in the courts would be an intrusion on the proceedings and damage the dignity if not the sanctity of the courts. Many jurists believed that the purpose of a trial was not to inform or educate the public but to conduct a rigorous search for truth and that court proceedings were designed to do just that. A camera, they believed, was an unnecessary addition to the judicial environment.

In 1917, the Illinois State Supreme Court became the first legal authority to advise state courts to bar cameras during trials. Until this decision, photojournalists had access to Illinois courts, although granting such access was left to the discretion of each judge. In 1925, forty-five Chicago judges voted to prohibit cameras in state courtrooms during judicial proceedings. Nonetheless, in other parts of the country judges were of mixed opinion about the appropriateness of allowing cameras into the courts. One of the most famous decisions in favor of having them was made by Judge John T. Raulston, who presided at the "monkey" trial of John Scopes in Dayton, Tennessee, in 1925. News photographers were allowed to take photographs during certain moments of the trial, including photographs of Clarence Darrow addressing the court. Radio broadcasts were also made from the courtroom, and the general atmosphere was far from dignified. Nonetheless, judicial opinion about the use of cameras still remained divided after the Scopes trial. In a Maryland murder case that followed two years later, a judge cited two photographers and three editors from Baltimore's *News American* for contempt after discovering that seven photographs had been taken surreptitiously during the first day of the trial. Two of the photographs were published the following day. The newspapers argued that while the judge had discretionary power, he could not ban cameras completely. But a court of appeals decision concluded that a judge could act to limit and even prohibit cameras in order to protect a defendant's rights and to maintain judicial decorum. The newspapers were forced to pay a fine of $5,000, and the five newsmen were sentenced to one day in jail.

The Maryland decision, however, did not settle the issue. The matter was decided, or so it seemed, in 1935 by the trial of Bruno Hauptmann, accused of kidnapping and murdering the baby of Charles and Anne Morrow Lindbergh. At that trial, in Flemington, New Jersey, Judge Thomas Trenchard allowed the use of both newsreel and still photography within the courtroom, although under some restrictions. For example, no filming was permitted when the judge was seated on the bench, but witnesses could repeat highlights of their testimony to photojournalists following court proceedings.

It is generally believed that the presence of photographers turned the courtroom into a circus, one popular commentator calling the scene "a Roman holiday." At one point, overzealous photographers made the judge decide to bar all photographic coverage in the courtroom. Ironically, a hidden newsreel camera took footage that was later shown in movie theaters all over the country.

As a result of the Hauptmann trial, the American Bar Association formed a special committee to study the issue. The committee urged a ban on cameras, expressed in a recommendation that came to be known as Canon 35. Canons of the

American Bar Association do not carry with them the force of law, but this one became the basis of legislation aimed at banning still and newsreel cameras and later, in 1952, TV cameras, from the courts. State legislatures, one after the other, codified the canon into state law so that by 1965 all states except Colorado and Texas had such laws. In fact, the first live TV broadcast of a trial took place in Waco, Texas, on December 6, 1955. The judge, of course, approved, but so did the jury and even the defendant, who was being tried for murder. The state of Colorado was equally lenient about cameras, and as a result of a petition by media representatives concerning the case of John Gilbert Graham (he was being tried for planting a bomb on an airplane, which killed forty-four people, including his mother), the court worked out an agreement that permitted cameras entry but with TV stations pooling their resources. Colorado, in fact, became the first state to allow TV cameras in state courtrooms with the permission of the presiding judge.

The traditional argument against allowing cameras in the courts was that they were, by their nature, intrusive; that is, they were distracting and noisy. These arguments weakened as media technologies improved, and, especially, as TV technology became less physically cumbersome. However, other arguments began to surface. For example, it was claimed that the presence of cameras could create psychological problems for judges, lawyers, witnesses, and juries. The argument for allowing cameras in the courts continued along the same lines used from the beginning: the press had an absolute right to cover trials as guaranteed by the First Amendment and to do so by using whatever tools of the trade were available. Thus, a constitutional conflict arose between a defendant's right to a fair trial and the First Amendment right of a free press. The American Bar Association tended toward the view that the defendant's rights outweighed the rights of the press and, in

1965, received support from a decision by the U.S. Supreme Court in the case of *Estes v. Texas*. Billy Sol Estes was a prominent political figure who had been convicted in a Texas courtroom in 1962 for fraudulent financial dealings. The trial judge, as was the predisposition in Texas courts, allowed photographers and TV cameras into the courtroom during pretrial hearings. The U.S. Supreme Court reversed Estes' conviction on the grounds that the televising of "notorious criminal trials" was a denial of the defendant's right to due process. In addition to citing the fact that the cameras had been a distraction, the Court, in a five-to-four ruling, made a broad condemnation of television claiming that the use of in-court cameras was itself unfriendly to the judicial process. The Court claimed cameras could corrupt a juror's impartiality, impair the testimony of witnesses, affect a judge's decisions, and subject the defendant to mental harassment.

But the press's continuing insistence that it was being denied its constitutional rights kept the door ajar. In 1977, the state of Florida broke the door down. In that year, a pilot project was begun, under the auspices of the State Supreme Court, allowing trials to be televised. Among the trials included in the pilot project was that of Ronny Zamora, a fifteen-year-old charged with murdering an eighty-two-year-old woman. The trial received national attention, not only because it was televised, but also because of Zamora's defense. He had been made insane, he claimed, by watching violent television programs. Presiding judge Paul Baker, who had originally been opposed to the pilot project, concluded by the end of the trial that the pilot experiment was a success; that is, it demonstrated that the courts and the electronic press can work harmoniously. The tide began to turn. In fact, in the following year, the U.S. Supreme Court in effect reversed itself on *Estes*. Two former Miami Beach policemen who had been found guilty of burglary, Noel Chandler and Robert Granger, appealed their conviction, arguing that the presence of TV cameras at their trial influenced the behavior of attorneys, witnesses, and jurors. They relied heavily on the Court's reasoning in *Estes*, but it didn't work. A considerable number of legal organizations, state chief justices, and state attorneys general filed briefs with the Court, maintaining that cameras in no way harmed the judicial process. The Supreme Court agreed, as did many state legislatures throughout the country. By the time *Chandler v. Florida* was decided, twenty-nine states had adopted rules allowing cameras on either a permanent or experimental basis. By April 1987, forty-three states had some form of rules permitting camera coverage during trials (although only twenty-seven states allowed coverage of criminal trials).

In December 1987, New York became the forty-fourth state to allow TV cameras into the courtroom. When the relevant law expired, cameras were barred from the courts. This debate has relevance beyond New York State. Keep in mind that in 1965 (the *Estes* case) it appeared cameras would be permanently barred from most courtrooms. That changed, but it can change again.

Because of our familiarity with the arguments, we can summarize the case for and against cameras in the courts. (One of us, Postman, was a member of a New York State advisory committee on cameras in the courts, whose function was to assess the competing evidence and points of view on the matter. Powers has used trial footage in his TV news stories.) Here's the way it stacks up:

1. Journalists and TV executives, especially of news departments, claim that the First Amendment to the Constitution gives them an absolute right to be in the courtroom with their cameras, provided, of course, that the cameras in no way disrupt the proceedings. If the print press can be there, the

electronic press can be there. It is even questionable that the electronic press has to await *permission* from a state legislature in order to gain entry. This, the argument goes, is none of the legislature's business. The First Amendment makes that clear. The only question to be decided is whether the cameras are a distraction. In the days of *Hauptmann* and even *Estes*, they might have been. But now a camera is only part of the furniture and is completely unobtrusive.

The reply to this argument usually begins with the word "nonsense." It goes on from there as follows: From 1927, when Congress passed the Radio Act, to 1934, when the federal Communications Act was passed, to the present, Congress and the courts have distinguished between print and broadcasting. Unlike a newspaper, which is *owned* by a person or corporation, a TV channel cannot be owned by anyone. The airwaves belong to the people, who lease a frequency, and who can revoke or otherwise deny a lease if the broadcaster does not operate the station in "the public interest, convenience, and necessity." *The New York Times*, for example, is not required to publish in the public interest, does not require a government license, and is not legally responsible to the "people." A TV station is. Therefore, the First Amendment does not give the electronic press absolute protection against government regulation or restrictions. If a legislature wishes to bar TV cameras from the courts, it may do so.

As for the question of the camera's intrusiveness, the evidence is not as clear as TV executives claim. It is difficult to know exactly how the presence of a TV camera alters the behavior of participants in a trial. Some research suggests that changes in behavior are minimal; a few studies indicate that both witnesses and lawyers are demonstrably affected by the presence of cameras. The argument against cameras claims that Chief Justice Earl Warren (in *Estes*) was right: any time you put cameras into a situation, you change the situation. Only further, more detailed, and more sophisticated research can tell us to what extent the situation is changed.

2. Those in favor of cameras in the courts also argue that television has enormous potential for educating the public (in the second meaning of the word). Surveys of the public's knowledge of the judicial system consistently reveal that most people know very little about the judicial process. One study uncovered the astonishing fact that roughly one third of those people who had *served on juries* did not know that a defendant is considered innocent until proven guilty. Such ignorance is unacceptable in a democratic society, and whatever can be done to eradicate it should be done. Television is an indispensable medium for enlarging public understanding of an essential institution.

The educational value of televising trials was stressed in the preamble to New York's law in 1987. The hope was expressed that the televising of trials would not only increase the public's knowledge of the courts but would also increase respect for the judicial process.

The reply to this is as follows: it doesn't. One study we know of that bears on the issue (by Dr. William Petkanas of New York University) reveals that after eighteen months of televised trials on New York State TV stations, the audience knew no more about the operation of the courts, and had no greater respect for the judicial process, than before trials were televised. The usual explanation for this is that TV stations never show a trial its entirety. In fact, they usually show a thirty- or sixty-second fragment of a trial, most often a dramatic moment. One of the ironic discoveries of the Petkanas study is that fictionalized trials (in *Boston Legal*, for example) seem to educate the public better than do actual trials. For example, most people in the survey knew that a defense lawyer is an "officer of the court." When queried as to how they knew this, most said that the fact is frequently mentioned on lawyer shows.

Conversely, of course, a major stumbling block to truly educating the public about the legal system is television's use of partial trial coverage as entertainment.

3. Another argument for including cameras is that our public institutions must learn to accommodate themselves to new technologies. It is reactionary and regressive to pretend that television does not exist. We cannot turn the clock back. Schools, businesses, theaters, the halls of Congress, political conventions, even ballparks have made adjustments to fit new technological possibilities. So must the courts.

In fact, over the centuries, the courts have done this. There was a time when law was entirely based on the oral tradition. With the invention of writing, then printing, law changed. Judges decide cases on the basis of *written precedent*. Lawyers' briefs are written documents. The courts have always reconceived their rules to exploit the advantages of new media of communication. Photographs are admitted as evidence; so are wiretaps and other recordings. In other words, the judicial process has never been indifferent to technological progress. Why stop television from doing what it can do?

Moreover, until recently the courts were largely a semi-public space, available only to those who could be physically present. The first television coverage of a court case is believed to have taken place in Oklahoma City, Oklahoma, in the 1953 criminal trial of Billy Eugene Manley. The first live broadcast of a trial occurred in 1955 when Harry L. Washburn was tried for murder in Waco, Texas.

Television converts the courts into public space. It doesn't matter if the public is educated or not by televised trials any more than it matters if the public is educated by seeing a televised press conference or political convention. Television is a window to the world. People will enjoy seeing that world or not, will learn from it or not. But it is there, and it makes no sense to say we will pull down the shades when it comes to trials.

The answer to these arguments is as follows: First, what's wrong with turning back the clock if the clock is wrong? We need not be slaves to our technologies. Every technological advance has its advantages and disadvantages. It is our job to control the uses of technology so that what is best about our culture can be preserved. Second, television does not turn trials into a public event but into a public spectacle. Let's be honest about this: what the public is shown is intended only to entertain them, even titillate them. TV stations are not, in fact, interested in showing trials but only in showing fragments of "sexy" trials, those that involve murder, rape, kidnapping, and other horrifying crimes. TV stations would, if they could, show the actual murders, rapes, and kidnappings. In fact, a San Francisco TV station petitioned to be allowed to televise an execution. Why? Not because it is good public policy, we suspect, but because it would draw a huge audience. Failing to televise actual deaths, TV must settle for the next best "show": a glimpse of a murderer on trial.

As for the courtroom being a semipublic space, that's exactly what it should be. Its rules have been worked out over centuries. The procedures are not perfect, but they are designed to give everyone a fair shake, and there is no good reason to alter them. And keep this in mind: reading about a trial and seeing it on television are two quite different experiences. A man who is found not guilty ordinarily may resume his life. A man who is found not guilty but who has been seen on television during his trial may find it impossible to resume his life. Audiences may even forget if he was found guilty or not.

In any case, he becomes notorious in one way or another, which is to say, he is tried twice: once in the courts and a second time in the court of public exposure.

Nowadays, the "hot" trial of the moment is featured with anchors/commentators guiding us through the proceedings. Critics fear that television coverage, in aiming for a wide general audience, will focus on the sensational, thus trivializing the court system. Recent history indicates that the public is interested in viewing courtroom proceedings if the subject of the trial is wrapped in celebrity and sensational detail. We don't even have to tell you the name of the defendant in the most publicized case in U.S. history—just his initials. O.J., as in O. J. Simpson. The cast of characters in the 1995 televised trial became as famous as any TV or movie star, including Judge Lance Ito, Marcia Clark, Johnnie Cochran, and Mark Fuhrman. One poll showed that 74 percent of Americans could identify an O.J. trial witness, Kato Kaelin, but only 25 percent knew who the vice president was at the time (Al Gore). The trial generated windfalls for attorneys Chris Darden, Marcia Clark, and Johnnie Cochran who all received large advances for writing books about the case. Police witness Mark Fuhrman cashed in with his own tome, and Nancy Grace parlayed her trial reporting into her own TV show. According to Court TV, an incredible 91 percent of the television viewing audience watched the O.J. trial and an unbelievable 142 million people listened on radio and watched television as the verdict was delivered. Two thousand reporters covered the trial.

Ten years later, another celebrity, actor Robert Blake, walked after his televised trial. Ratings were sky-high for the trial of Scott Peterson, a noncelebrity who became one because of his televised trial. After being convicted for murdering his pregnant wife, there were reports he received fan letters in prison, including marriage proposals. On the international scene, Iraqi dictator Saddam Hussein's trial got only sporadic coverage, but his execution on December 30, 2006, was a top-rated story, sensationalized by videotape of the actual hanging.

Despite the record, our own view is that opening the courtroom to the television eye might increase public understanding of the judicial system, but only if coverage extends beyond TV's need to dramatize the sensational moment.

CHAPTER 11

What Does It All Mean?

I N COMING TOWARD THE end of our book, we must address the question that is the title of this chapter. We will begin by saying something about children. No book about television—*any* aspect of television—can neglect doing so, since it is generally assumed that children are more vulnerable than adults to what may be confusing, destructive, or enriching about television. This assumption may not be valid, but there is no denying that children are the most avid group of TV viewers. In America, despite warnings from the American Academy of Pediatrics about the fact that 40 percent of three-month-olds watch TV or videos an average of forty-five minutes a day, or five hours a week, and children between the ages of two and twelve watch an average of twenty-five hours of television per week. The young ones watch about five thousand hours before entering the first grade, and by high school's end the average American youngster has clocked nineteen thousand hours in front of a TV set. The same youngster will have spent only thirteen thousand hours in school, assuming that he or she is regular in attendance. What it comes down to is that American children spend 30 percent of their waking hours in front of a television set. And that means exposure to roughly 13,000 killings, about 200,000 violent episodes, and somewhere in the neighborhood of 650,000 commercials by age eighteen. According to the American Academy of Pediatrics, children in the United States see 40,000 commercials each year.

Given all this, it can come as no surprise, to say the least, that our youngsters know more about Dr. Dre on MTV, or even Dr. Phil, than *Doctor Zhivago* and that their heads are full of jingles about McDonald's, Coca-Cola, and products from Disney's *High School Musical*. It should be noted, by the way, that one in four TV commercials seen by teens is a food ad, according to a University of Illinois study. The most common ads were for fast food, beverages, and sweets. If our children know more about munchies and crunchies than about how much protein they need for healthy nutrition every day, no one need be astonished.

For quite a long time, scholars have attempted to discover exactly what effects television has on our young. Because television is by no means the only factor influencing the minds of our youth, it is not easy to pin this down. Some studies indicate that children who watch a lot of TV tend to spend less time outdoors and don't play with friends as much as children who are light viewers. In its 2003 policy statement, the American Academy of Pediatrics concluded that too much TV can make children fat since TV viewing is a sedentary activity. Concerned that a steady diet of TV ads is putting too many pounds on American children, the FCC is studying links between ads, viewing habits, and the rise of childhood obesity. In September 2006, FCC chairman Kevin Martin said, "Small children can't weed out the marketing messages from their favorite shows. . . . Especially when the marketing campaigns feature favorite TV characters like Sponge Bob or Scooby-Doo." Martin cited reports showing that the average child watches two to four hours of TV per day and views about forty thousand TV ads every year, most of them for cereal, candy, toys, and fast food. There are even some studies indicating that children who view a lot of television do less well in school than light viewers. According to a 2007 study published in the journal *Pediatrics*, watching television more than two hours a day early in life can lead to attention problems later in adolescence. The research showed that there was a 40 percent increase in attention problems among heavy TV viewers in both boys and girls.

One of the more comprehensive studies, supported by the National Institute of Mental Health, is worth mentioning. The investigators, Robert Kubey of Rutgers and Mihaly Csikszent-mihalyi (pronounced Schwartz) of the University of Chicago, were not primarily interested in TV's effects on children but uncovered enough data to lead them to suggest that children be educated in the art of TV watching so that they will be less easily manipulated. Their research spanned thirteen years and involved 1,200 subjects in nine different studies. Their conclusion: television makes people passive, tense, and unable to concentrate; more skill and concentration are required in the act of eating than in watching television; although people assume that TV watching offers relaxation and escape, it actually leaves people in worse moods than they were in before watching television.

There are, of course, many studies focusing on the effects of TV violence on children—at last count about three thousand—many of them ambiguous. Nonetheless, after reviewing the data, the American Academy of Pediatrics concluded that TV violence "promotes a proclivity to violence and a passive response to its practice. . . . Kids who view violent events, such as kidnapping or murder, are also more likely to believe the world is scary and that something bad will happen to them." In April 2007, the FCC recommended that Congress craft an anti-violence law that would not run afoul of free-speech rights and would protect children. The FCC said such a law is necessary because studies show that children's extended exposure to TV violence can lead to more aggressive behavior.

Which brings us to TV news. TV news is now more accessible to children than ever. News shows are on the air from early morning until late at night, and there is no lack of realism in their depictions of the violence in the human condition. Rapes, muggings, terrorism, and drug-related murders and kidnappings are the currency of the evening news. And with the proliferation of pseudonews tabloid shows, young eyes can feast on wall-to-wall horror, and the horror can feast on young minds. During sweeps periods, when a television station has its audience measured, sordid subjects of every known variety, and a few that were previously unknown, are wheeled out, advertised, and featured to attract an audience. In February 2007, WTAE's Kelly Frey "reported" a story on "a new exercise craze": pole dancing. You could have argued that it was a legitimate feature about a new fad—until Kelly got on the pole herself. The segment probably was appreciated by the audience, but don't forget the audience included children. Here we come to the heart of a major problem. By contrast with other media (e.g., books, newspapers, magazines), television is an "open-admission" technology. It does not require reading skills. It is largely free. It is activated by the turn of a switch. Its programs are designed to gratify emotions immediately. It is more than friendly to its users. It adores them. As a consequence, the six-year-old and the sixty-year-old are equally vulnerable to what TV has to offer. Television, in this sense, is the consummate egalitarian medium of communication, surpassing oral language itself. For in speaking, we may always whisper so that the children will not hear. Or we may use words they may not understand. But television cannot whisper, and its pictures are concrete and vivid. Children see everything TV reveals.

The most obvious effect of this situation is that it eliminates the exclusivity of worldly knowledge. This means that the knowledge that distinguishes adults from children; that is, the "secrets" of adult life—political secrets, sexual secrets, medical secrets, and so on—are now constantly in view, including the extent to which human beings are prone to violence. In an earlier time, it was possible, within limits, to keep this knowledge from children, which was done for a perfectly good reason: too much of such knowledge, too soon, is considered dangerous to the well-being of an unformed mind. Enlightened opinion on child development claims it is necessary for children to believe that adults have control over their impulses to violence and have a clear conception of right and wrong. Through these beliefs children develop positive feelings about themselves that give them strength to nurture their rationality, which, in turn, will sustain them in adversity. But TV undermines this entire process. And here we must keep in mind that the stylized murders, rapes, and plundering depicted on weekly fictional programs are much less than half the problem. Such programs are, after all, understood to be fiction or pseudo–fairy tales, and we may assume (although not safely) that some children do not take them to be representations of real adult life. Far more significant are the daily examples of violence and moral degeneracy that are the staple of TV news shows. These are not mitigated by the presence of recognizable and attractive actors and actresses. They are put forward as the stuff of everyday life. These are real murders, real rapes, real plundering. And the fact that they are the stuff of real life makes them all the more powerful.

What are the long-range effects on children of their seeing mayhem and adult incompetence every night on TV news?
No one can be sure. Some say that the effect may be positive
in that children will develop a more realistic sense of what life
is like. The argument is made that the traditional manner of
socializing children is hypocritical. We do not live in a Mary
Poppins world, and the sooner children know this, the better.
But it seems to us that hypocrisy should be made of sterner
stuff. If it is hypocrisy to conceal from children the "facts" of
adult violence and moral ineptitude, it is nonetheless wise
to do so. Surely, hypocrisy in the cause of fostering healthy
psychological development in children is no vice.

But it is probably useless to debate this issue. The plain
facts are these: television operates around the clock; its audiences cannot be segregated; parental supervision of television
viewing has proved ineffectual; and programs, especially TV
news, require a continuous supply of novel information to en-
gage the audience. Thus television must make use of every existing taboo in the culture, including sexual perversity, irrational
violence, insanity, and the ineptitude of political leaders. Taboos
may be discussed on talk shows, soap operas, commercials, or
news shows. How the information gets to the audience is irrelevant. Television needs material, for its business is to *move*
information, not collect it. And as long as the present system
of competitive, commercial broadcasting exists, this situation
will also exist. We suspect that if every network executive and
program director were replaced tomorrow by, say, the faculty
of the Harvard Divinity School, TV programming, including
TV news shows, would remain quite close to what it is.

One might think, therefore, that in the face of this some
attempts would be made to shield children from news shows
or at least to provide them with a different vision of the news.
In fact, there have been some attempts to design TV news

specifically for children. At least two shows are produced to be played right in the classroom. Turner Broadcasting produces a ten-minute news program for children called *CNN Student News*, and it comes without commercial interruption. The CNN newscast is broadcast on CNN *Headline News* at 3:12 a.m. eastern standard time to be recorded for playback in classrooms. In addition, the program is available on the Internet and on video podcasts. On the other hand, *Channel One*, produced by Primedia, presents newscasts complete with commercials. Participating schools are given $50,000 worth of TV monitors, VCRs, and a satellite dish in exchange for requiring students to watch the program. The show consists of ten minutes of news and two minutes of commercials including ads for foods, soft drinks, and movies. The four thirty-second spots cost advertisers $150,000 each. Primedia claims that *Channel One* reaches 30 percent of U.S. teens. *Channel One* has been banned by some states, including New York, on the grounds that it exploits a trapped audience, children, under the guise of presenting an educational program. The claim is made that the shows are too simplistic, are too fast paced to allow much development, and are merely cynical attempts to take advantage of gullible children. Other educators claim that news shows in the classroom make civics lessons come alive and open the door to interesting classroom discussions. The former president of Action for Children's Television, Peggy Charren, has criticized *Channel One* for encouraging consumerism in teenagers even while they are in a learning environment. Primedia, of course, defends its newscasts and notes that newspapers and magazines that carry advertising are routinely used in schools; even soda machines in schools are advertisements of sorts.

While it is true that the school environment is not a commercial-free zone, the question remains: should students be "for sale" to the highest bidder? The stakes are high. *Channel*

One claims it reached seven million students by the end of 2006—earning hundreds of millions of advertising dollars—and, in that same year, the American Academy of Pediatrics reported that children who watched *Channel One* tended to remember the commercials more than the news.

Apparently, there will be no relief from the news wherever we go, and that leads us to a problem that all of us must face, not only children. One way to express the problem is by recalling a remark made by the American novelist Philip Roth. In commenting on the difference between being a novelist in the West and being a novelist behind the iron curtain (this was before the collapse of Communism in Eastern Europe), Roth said that in Eastern Europe nothing is permitted but everything matters; with us, everything is permitted but nothing matters. The observation may no longer apply to the work of novelists, but it does apply to the news business. We have here, in other words, a paradox of sorts. The more information, the less significant information is. The less information, the more significant it is. There is nothing so unusual about this. Perhaps it is a law of human nature. To a man with fifty suits, one suit is not so important. To a man with one suit, that suit is everything. We are, of course, not making an argument for denying people access to information. But we are calling attention to the problem known as "information glut." Put simply, it is this: as our news media, especially television, fill our days with information from everywhere, about everything, we have increasing difficulty in deciding what any of it means. We do not have time to reflect on any piece of news, and we are rarely helped, least of all by television itself, to know what weight or value to assign to any of it. We become information junkies, addicted to news, demanding (even requiring) more and more of it, but without any notion of what to do with it. One extremely minor example of "news," reported by

Anderson Cooper on CNN and others in April 2007, was the problem actor Alec Baldwin was having communicating with his daughter. His rant at his daughter for not taking his phone call was recorded on an answering machine and apparently released to the news media by his ex-wife, actress Kim Basinger. Newscasters breathlessly played the tape of the father angry with his daughter. This is major news?

Television, we need to say, did not start all this. The roots of information glut are to be found in the mid-nineteenth century with the invention of the telegraph and photograph. There followed, over the next century, a dazzling demonstration of technological ingenuity that gave us the rotary press, radio, telephone, motion pictures, and computers, in addition to television. This development is usually called "the communications revolution," sometimes "the information explosion." Marshall McLuhan, the first "media guru" of our age, claimed that the electronic world in which we now live has created a "global village," in which everything has become everyone's business. McLuhan probably never lived in a village; if he had, he might have used a different metaphor for our present situation. In a village, information is apt to be a precious commodity. Villagers seek information that directly affects their lives, and they usually know what to do with it when they get it. Villagers may like gossip, as it adds a certain zest to life, but they can usually distinguish between gossip and information that materially affects their lives. Our relation to information is quite different. For us, information is a commodity. It is bought and sold. Most of it has little to do with our lives. And most of the time, we don't know what to do with it.

We can, of course, use information as entertainment, as, for example, during the Gulf War. Viewers were witnesses to the first attack on Baghdad in 1990, as the United States and other U.N. forces launched their offensive. Ironically, this amazing television first was in audio form only: journalists in their hotel rooms telephoned their reports to CNN in Atlanta. Subsequently, satellite uplinks brought war into living rooms around the world. Network correspondents covering the war were admonished not give too much detail about the ensuing battles because information might help the enemy, who was watching television, too. Many Americans got out of their beds at 4:00 a.m. eastern standard time to watch the noon briefings in Saudi Arabia. The commander of the allied forces, General Norman Schwarzkopf, showed videos of "smart bombs" and described battle strategies, thus allowing viewers to know exactly, and at the same instant, what the reporters covering the briefings could know. Viewers also witnessed the seriocomic scenes of TV reporters diving for cover as air-raid sirens went off during their stand-ups. Viewers saw live reports as Kuwait City was liberated, heard incoming Scud missile attacks on Israel and Saudi Arabia, and watched as Iraqis surrendered and the wounded were brought to hospitals. The eyewitness video lens made newspapers, with their day-old coverage, stale.

All of this, you will remember, was presented as a kind of show, a drama that entertained as much as anything else. There were heroes and villains; there were acts and scenes; there were comedic episodes: during the U.S. war in Afghanistan in 2001, Geraldo Rivera claimed to be at the scene of a friendly fire incident, but it was later revealed he was actually three hundred miles away. In the nineties, each network, incredibly, had a theme song to introduce news about the war ("The Desert Song"?). The play had a name. In fact, two names: Desert Shield then Desert Storm. Today, it's the War on Terror. We've come to wars as we would a miniseries, and, as it turned out in the Gulf War, a good one at that. Its last act was entirely satisfactory, allowing for parades celebrating the glorious re-turn of the warriors. General Schwarzkopf was able to retire as a millionaire, with a book contract and, of course, a lucrative career as a TV commentator and lecturer. In the Iraq war, the drama played out differently. At first, viewers were treated to a daily episode of embedded adventures as troops were welcomed, statues were toppled, and Saddam's troops were vanquished. Then the daily TV feeding frenzy came to an end as the fighting intensified, driving American journalists into the safety of the Green Zone. With the battlefield coverage cut off, and even pictures of the combat dead in coffins denied, the TV audience was deprived of its dose of video adrenalin and the opportunity to anoint a new hero. Action was replaced by Washington talking heads. The war in Iraq goes on, and most people can no longer follow the day-to-day adventures. Un-fortunately, wars are not like TV shows and cannot be canceled for lack of viewer interest.

We do not say, by the way, that the war was unjustified. That would be the subject of a different book. We are saying that television tends to turn its news into a form of entertain-ment, in part because so much information is available that news has lost its relevance and meaning. Americans are no longer clear about what news is worth remembering or how any of it is connected to anything else. As a consequence, Americans have rapidly become the least knowledgeable people in the industrialized world. We know *of* many things (everything is revealed) but *about* very little (nothing is known).

In intellectual achievement and historical knowledge, American students are several tiers below students in other countries, and no one, apparently, knows why. It has not yet occurred to our education leaders that our students, like the rest of us, are suffering from information glut. They do not yet acknowledge that it is impossible to read the writing on a wall if, every day, new words are written over the old ones. The writing soon loses its coherence and becomes a jumble. After a while, the wall may become an object of aesthetic contemplation, people may enjoy looking at it, but it will be worthless as a medium of rational expression; that is, as a means of organizing one's knowledge.

There are some critics and scholars who take a different view of all this. For example, Henry Perkinson, in *Getting Better: Television and Moral Progress*, opines that the proliferation of images, especially on television news shows, tends to make viewers more sensitive to the sufferings of other people. Television news allowed us to see, for example, the face of the enemy during the Vietnam War; it showed us the pain and humiliation of blacks being beaten in our own country, of students being shot in China, of children starving in Ethiopia, of Russians resisting an illegal coup. The cumulative effect of all this has been to widen our moral universe and connect us emotionally with people who, before television, were merely abstract "others." In his book, Perkinson provides examples of what he sees as a historical evolution of morals as humankind has progressed from speech to writing to printing to television. We recommend his book, especially to those who are chronically depressed. As for us, we find the evidence for moral improvement difficult to find and, when found, even more difficult to believe.

We would respond in the same way to the contention that the images provided by TV news serve to bind the nation and provide a sense of national purpose. There is no denying that funerals of political leaders, scenes of hostages being released, the horrific vision of astronauts being blown out of the sky, and the joy or anguish of a record-setting home run are fixed in the consciousness of American TV viewers. These events and their accompanying imagery certainly provide us with material for conversation, but it is not yet demonstrable that shared images make for shared purposes or even shared understandings. In fact, a quite opposite trend is under way. We refer to the return to "tribalism," as different ethnic, racial, and religious groups aggressively reject the metaphor of the melting pot. They insist on the supremacy of their unique identities and demand that our social, political, and educational systems recognize the reality of "multiculturalism." In Britain in October 2006, tribalism, in the form of costume, became a major political issue. The question was whether a woman could wear a kerchief-size item of Islamic dress called the *niqab*, a full-face veil. Prime minister Tony Blair called the veil "a mark of separation." People who long favored tolerance for individual choice called for the rejection of tribalism in favor of integration into a larger group. Along with Mr. Blair's comment, a Conservative opposition figure, David Davis, said some British Muslims had set themselves on a course of "voluntary apartheid," leading parallel lives outside the mainstream. The inference was that multiculturalism had failed. In other words, if TV's images have enriched our sense of a shared national heritage, it is not yet manifest.

We take no pleasure in seeming so pessimistic. That television, and in particular TV news, might be an intellectually enriching and morally ennobling enterprise is devoutly to be wished—by us, as well as anyone else. Who knows? It might yet be. But we are trying to be realistic, and such optimism as we have is reserved for the next chapter, where we indicate what you may do to defend yourself against the negative influence of TV news and to maximize what is useful.

CHAPTER 12

What Can You Do?

BELOW WE HAVE LISTED eight recommendations, with accompanying commentaries, which you may find useful in adjusting your relation to TV news shows or in helping others to do so. We have not included among them the most effective strategy, which is to move to Switzerland. Some people have thought of this, but the Swiss are very particular about who they let in, so it is impractical. Those recommendations that follow are, we believe, well within the competence of anyone who has come this far in our book.

1. In encountering a news show, you must come with a firm idea of what is important.

Even an "open mind" has to have boundaries, and you will be endlessly manipulated if you have no clear basis for evaluating the significance of "news." Remember: TV is not what happened. It is what some man or woman who has been labeled a journalist or correspondent thinks is worth reporting. You may agree or not, but it is your business to judge the importance of what is reported. Journalists would prefer you to trust them. Walter Cronkite did a disservice to viewers by concluding his famous CBS nightly news program with the words "And that's the way it was on this day..." What he meant to say, and should have said, is "And that's the way our gang on Fifty-seventh Street thought things were on this day..."

We suggest that if you form your own notions of what is worth reporting, you will not be so easily manipulated by the choices of TV news directors and journalists. Of course, the question of how one develops a sense of what is significant is very complex, well beyond the scope of our book and also beyond our competence. But obviously, family background and, especially, education play an important role. If we were to write a book on education, we would certainly stress the point that our schools have apparently abandoned the task of helping youngsters construct a moral and political belief system to help guide them in knowing what is important.

2. In preparing to watch a TV news show, keep in mind that it is called a "show."

You may think that a TV news show is a public service and a public utility. But more than that, it is an enormously successful business enterprise. This does not mean that it is of no value. It means: first, that the "news" is only a commodity, which is used to gather an audience that will be sold to advertisers; second, that the "news" is delivered as a form of entertainment (or at least, theater) because audiences find this palatable; and third, that the whole package is put together in the way that any theatrical producer would proceed; that is, by giving priority to show business values. In the case of most news shows, the package includes attractive anchors, an exciting musical theme, comic relief (usually from the weather people, especially the men), stories placed to hold the audience, the creation of the illusion of intimacy, and so on. The point of this kind of show is that *no one is expected to take the news too seriously*. For one thing, tomorrow's news will have nothing to do with today's news. It is, in fact, best if the audience has completely forgotten yesterday's news. TV shows work best by treating viewers as if they were amnesiacs.

3. Never underestimate the power of commercials.

As we have emphasized, commercials are not fluff. They are a serious form of popular literature, some would even say a serious form of news. Upon being asked if TV news is always bad news, Marshall McLuhan once remarked that it is not; the commercials, he said, are the good news. However we may label them, commercials tell as much about our society as "straight" news does, probably more. We suspect that archaeologists studying the artifacts of American culture two hundred years from now will find our commercials the richest source of information about our fears, motivations, and exultations. In any case, it is always of special interest for a viewer to observe the contradictions between the messages of commercials and the messages of the news. In these contradictions, we may glimpse, pure if not serene, the social and psychic dilemmas of our culture.

4. Learn something about the economic and political interests of those who run TV stations.

This is not easy to do since it requires one to read industry publications, the *Wall Street Journal, Advertising Age*, and other related sources of information. But since we are going to suggest that you reduce by one third your viewing of TV news (recommendation 6), you might use the time saved to familiarize yourself with the backgrounds of those who are constructing the world for you. Keep in mind that other professionals—doctors, dentists, and lawyers, for example— commonly display their diplomas on their office walls to assure their clients that someone judged them to be competent. Granted, diplomas don't tell you much. (After all, half the doctors in America were, by definition, in the lower half of their graduating class.) But diplomas tell more than station "owners" and news directors and journalists tell. Wouldn't it be useful to know who these people are? Where they come from? What their angle is? And, especially, where they stand in relation to you? One doesn't have to be a Marxist to assume that people making $1 million a year will see things differently from people struggling to make ends meet.

Our intention is not to encourage paranoia. We only wish to stress the point that the background of those who deliver the news to us is relevant to how we will judge what they say. At the very least, you ought to give some thought to who owns the networks and some of the more important cable stations.

5. Pay special attention to the language of newscasts.

Because the film footage and other visual imagery on TV news shows are so engaging, viewers are apt to allow language to go unexamined. This is a mistake for several reasons, the most important of which is that a TV newscaster's language frames the pictures. As we have previously pointed out, a picture is by its nature a specific representation. However, what we are to make of the picture is often determined by the commentary made about it. Therefore, what is said requires careful attention. Since there are very few images that are self-explanatory, the viewer's attitude toward an image will be formed by words. There are limits, of course. A picture of a starving child cannot be converted into anything pleasant no matter how many words are used. But what the picture means must await commentary. Does the picture reflect the neglect of parents? The incompetence of politicians? The breakdown of an economic system? The callousness of the rich? These and other questions will be answered by the reporter's language. But this does not mean the explanation he or she gives is correct.

Another reason for attending to language is that reporters ask a lot of questions. A question is, after all, only a sentence. But it is a sentence that may reveal the biases and assumptions of the questioner as much as those of the person answering the question. For example, Fox News anchor Brit Hume asked why journalists should bother covering civilian deaths at all in the Iraq war. Hume said: "The question I have is civilian casualties are historically, by definition, a part of war, really. Should they be as big news as they've been?" In reply, the news watchdog group FAIR asked, "If journalists shouldn't cover civilian deaths because they are a normal part of war, does that principle apply to all war coverage? Dropping bombs is also standard procedure in a war; will Fox stop reporting airstrikes?" FAIR went on to label the Fox News Channel "The most biased name in news" for what it called "its extraordinary right-wing tilt."

Of course, when there is no war and news is of a less serious nature, viewers are apt to let their guard down and pay little attention to the nature of the questions asked. Don't let this happen.

6. Reduce by at least one third the amount of TV news you watch.

In considering this suggestion, you might keep in mind the case of Ronny Zamora, whom we had occasion to mention in the chapter on television and the courts. Ronny's defense against the charge of murdering an old woman was that he was driven insane by watching too much violence on television. The jury rejected his claim, but there is some value in your considering it. The Gerbner studies, also referred to before, clearly indicate that heavy viewing of TV news makes people think the world is much more dangerous than it actually is. The Kubey study indicates that watching television, including news shows, makes people somewhat more depressed than would otherwise be. While habitual viewing of TV may not make you insane, some believe it could turn you into a chronically depressed and constantly alarmed person.

Furthermore, if you are concerned that cutting down viewing time will cause you to "miss" important news, keep this in mind: each day's TV news consists, for the most part, of fifteen or so examples of one or the other of the seven deadly sins, with which you are already quite familiar. There may be a couple of stories exemplifying lust, usually four about murder, occasionally one about gluttony, another about envy, and so on. It cannot possibly do you any harm to excuse yourself each week from acquaintance with thirty or forty of these examples. Remember: TV news does not reflect normal, everyday life.

7. Reduce by one third the number of opinions you feel obligated to have.

One of the reasons many people are addicted to watching TV news is that they feel under pressure to have an opinion about almost everything. Middle-class people, at least those who are college educated, seem especially burdened by an unrealistic and slightly ridiculous obligation to have a ready-made opinion on any matter. For example, suppose you are attending a dinner party and someone asks you if you think the earth is undergoing permanent warming as a result of the increase in carbon dioxide emissions. You are expected to say something like, "Absolutely. In fact, I heard a discussion of this on CNN (or MSNBC or Fox News or even *Entertainment Tonight*) last Thursday, and it looks as if we're in for devastating climatic changes. I heard Al Gore got an Oscar for his movie about it." The fact is that you really don't know much about this matter, and TV coverage only provides the most rudimentary and fragmented information about anything. Wouldn't it be liberating to be able to say, when asked such a question, "I have no opinion on this since I know practically nothing about it"? Of course, we realize that if you gave such an answer five or six times during the course of a dinner party, you would probably not be asked back. But that would be a small price to pay for relieving yourself of the strain of storing thirty-two half-baked opinions to be retrieved at a moment's notice.

8. Do whatever you can to get schools interested in teaching children how to watch a TV news show.

The best thing about *Channel One* is that it provides teachers with an opportunity to teach about news shows, about the subjects we have addressed in this book. It is surely not Primedia's intention that TV news be made into an object of study, and it is doubtful that teachers wish to do so. Nonetheless, it is not merely a good idea to do it, it is essential. The best way to prepare ourselves to know exactly what is happening (and why) when we watch a TV news show is to begin learning about it all when we are young. For reasons that defy understanding, our schools have not been enthusiastic about making inquiries into any aspect of television. Generally, teachers are willing to use television as an aid to learning (which is what Primedia wants them to do), but they have not been willing to study how television uses us. Anything you can do to reverse this disposition will be helpful. Of course, we would have no serious objections to your recommending our book.

CHAPTER 13

Where Do We Go from Here?

IN TRADITIONAL OR OLD TV journalism, the gatekeepers in newsrooms decided what was important or interesting, and some of that news was put on the tube. The number of editor-deciders increased as the number of networks and local stations increased as cable came on line. News was suddenly available 24-7, via outlets such as CNN with live pictures from around the world, and with it came instant decision making about what content was sent into homes, packaged as news. The neatly framed network news, which organized our view of the world, was forced to change.

The news paradigm shifted again just as suddenly with the advent of the digital delivery of information. A wild dance of zeros and ones shot through wires made of metal and glass and sped through space not just to our television screens but to an array of devices. The BlackBerry, Palm Pilot, iPhone, satellite TV, cell phones, and PDAs bombard us with info pixels. Now, instead of information only flowing one way from the gatekeepers to the public, the news poured onto the Internet and spread like a blot absorbed by the world. A video shot by someone's cell phone camera could be uploaded, downloaded, viewed, edited, remixed, posted, and shown on TV. The one-way news flow had been splintered into fragments, all of them available for kaleidoscopic interpretations. Politicians could talk directly to voters without tough questioning from reporters. In 2007, Hillary Rodham Clinton, Bill Richardson, Barack Obama, and others announced their interest in running for the presidential nomination on the Internet. Why was there no announcement at a podium with a colorful flag behind them? Instead of fanfare and an authoritarian setting, they chose softer, more intimate surroundings where they didn't have to raise their voice and make lofty speeches. They controlled the time, the setting, the lighting, and, most important, enjoyed direct communication with their constituents without bothersome questions from journalists. Politicians can now talk to their audiences directly using Internet video, blogs, podcasts, diaries, links to social networks like MySpace and Facebook, chatrooms, and cell phones.

Of course, the elimination of the middlemen, the gatekeepers of network news, has its risks. On January 17, 2007, the Web site Insight, which is owned by an arm of the Reverend Sun Myung Moon's Unification Church, posted an article asserting that the presidential campaign of Hillary Rodham Clinton was preparing an accusation that her rival Senator Barack Obama had covered up a brief period he had spent in a radical Islamic religious school in Indonesia when he was six. *The New York Times* reported a confirmation of Mr. Obama's description of the school as a secular public school. Both senators denounced the report, and there was no evidence that Mrs. Clinton's campaign planned to spread the accusations. Despite the discrediting of the information on the Web site, commentators on the Fox News network devoted extensive discussions to Insight's assertion, as did Rush Limbaugh and other conservative talk-show hosts. The madrasa story was debunked by the Associated Press and CNN, which sent a reporter to check out the school. CNN anchor Anderson Cooper said: "That's the difference between talking about news and reporting it. You send a reporter, check the facts, and you decide at home."

The conventional concept of news is, perhaps, no longer valid. Narrowcasting has become "microcasting." An army of citizen journalists uses technology to post their stories, sound, pictures, and thoughts for mass consumption. YouTube visitors watched 100 million videos a day in 2006, all videos shot by ordinary folks and posted on the Web site. Admittedly, the content wasn't all Pulitzer prize material: Japanese lingerie commercials were mixed with footage of fighting in Iraq, sports bloopers, and music videos.

However, important events *are* captured. In November 2006, when comedian Michael Richards had a meltdown onstage in a comedy club in Los Angeles and used an offensive racist epithet, a video shot by an audience member promptly made its way onto TMZ.com, and the video spread like wildfire. The next month, another cell-phone video brought the world pictures of Saddam Hussein's hanging. On July 7, 2005, the most dramatic photos of the London terrorist bombing were taken by subway riders with cell phones and posted before news photographers could even get to the scene. The same was true when the tsunami hit South Asia in 2004 and amateur videos captured the vast devastation. Senator George Allen of Virginia lost his 2006 reelection bid, some believe, because of his use of a racial slur, *macaca*, for dark-skinned North Africans—comments that were videotaped and widely distributed on YouTube, newscasts, and elsewhere. The point is that suddenly the average person has a way to share homemade news with the rest of the world without going through a gatekeeper.

The two-way street of news gathering and disbursal is not just limited to videos, either. Internet users can now access news from around the world: newspapers in France, videos from Africa, articles from Iceland, wherever. Blogs, with the opinions of anyone who wants to post one—a teacher, a truck driver, a news anchor, whoever—can be put online around the globe with the stroke of a computer key. According to a study by the Pew Internet & American Life Project, there were 12 million bloggers in the United States alone in June 2006, and 34 percent of them consider blogging to be a form of journalism. You don't need a printing press. You don't need paper and ink. You don't need a deep-pocket publisher or an editor. You simply need access to a computer and the Internet.

This uncontrolled flow of billions of news bytes is causing friction with paper-bound newspapers who are feeling the heat of advertising jumping the divide from analog to digital. Newspapers such as the *New York Times* are moving their product toward an electronic "Continuous News" operation with constantly updated stories, pictures, videos, podcasts, interviews, journalist's blogs, and even obituaries. On January 18, 2007, the *Times* carried a video with columnist Art Buchwald in a prerecorded obituary. His opening statement: "Hi, I'm Art Buchwald and I just died." Talk about immediacy.

Television networks and local stations are also trying to move their products onto the Internet. NBC News was the first among the three big networks to put *NBC Nightly News* onto the Web and also has an *Early Nightly* video blog. Katie Couric offers a "web-exclusive rundown on-camera from the newsroom." *CBS Evening News* is simulcast on the Web. ABC's *World News with Charles Gibson* has dropped the word *tonight* from the 6:30 news broadcast to reflect the fact that it also has a webcast and blog. ABC News creates a fifteen-minute daily newscast, separate from *World News*, on its Web site and offers it on iTunes about an hour later, with millions of hits a month. The ABC webcast is aimed at a younger audience with a faster pace and more relaxed presentation. *ABC News Now,* a twenty-four-hour digital news service, is a digital suite of news content, with distribution on multiple media platforms including cable, satellite, broadband, and wireless. Viewers can submit text and video comments.

The amount and variety of the platforms now serving news is staggering. Besides world events, local cable channels run town zoning board and council meetings. In fact, a Pasadena-based online community newspaper advertised for a journalist based in India to report on Pasadena's local government and political scene. The idea was for the India-based "reporter" to watch the local board meetings over the Internet and then write them up for the newspaper at bargain rates. The editor/publisher, James Macpherson, says it doesn't matter if you're in Pasadena or Mumbai, "you're still just a phone call or e-mail away from an interview." A journalism professor at USC who lives in Pasadena calls it a "truly sad picture of what American journalism could become."

CBS Evening News with Katie Couric is simulcast on the Internet every evening, as well as broadcast on some radio stations. CBS is supplying YouTube with a variety of short-form video programming, including news, and they'll share advertising revenue. Yahoo! News, MSNBC.com, AOL News, CNN .com, and Google News offer a mix of text and video news content; Apple's iTunes Store carries video news and documentary programming. There are Web sites devoted exclusively to politics, state government affairs, journalism watchdogging, and the like, ad infinitum. RSS (really simple syndication) readers allow users to personalize the news by choosing subjects that will be gathered from many Web sites and displayed on their RSS reader. Interested in what's going on in Placitas, New

Mexico? Google will alert you when a news item you're interested in is published on the Internet, and other services like CBS News Mobile Web will bring the news to your phone in video or text. There are even sites, such as KNBC's in Los Angeles, that allow viewers to watch part of the morning in-house meeting and debriefs with producers, managers, and reporters about the day's news. The so-called *News Raw* also features behind-the-scenes chats with reporters on assignments. You can watch a weekly video podcast or vodcast (video on demand) of the BBC's *Ten O'Clock News*. NY1's *The Call* allows viewers to program the newscast the same way producers do: by ranking the importance of the day's news stories using a computer-generated rundown. In 2006, CNN became the first cable network to launch a site for receiving material from citizens, and since then more than one hundred thousand videos and pictures have been submitted by I-Reporters. Other networks and local stations have followed suit and offer similar interactive features: Fox started a similar site in 2007 and in the first six months its uReport program received forty thousand videos and pictures; MSNBC has received twenty-eight thousand submissions after starting its FirstPerson site in 2007. The Web site Digg promotes itself as being all about user-powered content. Users can post stories, videos, and podcasts; everything is submitted and voted on by the Digg community. There are no editors. The InfoLab at Northwestern University has developed a virtual news show. Totally autonomous, it collects, edits, and organizes news stories, then sends the formatted content to an artificial anchor for presentation. Presumably, graphic artists will be able to create the perfect anchor for your taste, along with the kinds of news stories you want to see and hear, when you want to view them, and in whatever medium you choose. One from column A and one from column B. You can make substitutions. Hold the soy sauce.

On top of all the technological breakthroughs, news has found a new young audience on comedy shows such as *The Daily Show with Jon Stewart*. In fact, Indiana University assistant professor of telecommunications Julia R. Fox did a study in 2006 that shows *The Daily Show* was as substantive as network news shows when it came to stories about the presidential election.

With the onslaught of news sources—both humorous and straight—it's no wonder that the network nightly news audience has dropped from 53 million to 27 million in the past twenty-five years. Did you get the picture? The audio? The text? Of course you did, and in an amazing number of ways. And that, friends, is the problem facing television news programs. Simply put, the programs are being overwhelmed by new news-delivery systems, and the systems are multiplying every day.

In 2001, the state-of-the-art transistor was approximately .25 microns. In 2006, it was .1 microns. In January 2007, Intel announced a breakthrough in the capacity and size of its transistors: approximately four hundred of its new 45-nanometer transistors could fit on the surface of a single human red blood cell. Consider that the number of transistors in a chip roughly doubles every two years. What does that mean? Computing will become even more powerful, less expensive, and so much more efficient that mobile devices like cell phones may soon accomplish tasks reserved until recently for desktop computers and other equipment with larger processors. Cell phones would be able to play full-length films, access news sites, and utilize new forms of information delivery that haven't yet been conceived. Implanted chips, anybody? News projected on your eyeglasses? Audio capsules in your ears? Three-dimensional content? Who needs the 6:30 network news? Who needs happy-talk anchors on pretty sets or funny weather people?

How will they fit on a nanoscreen? Why wait for the weather report on the 6:00 p.m. news when you can access any number of weather forecasts on the Internet in seconds?

In short, television news as we know it is endangered. It will be blown up by an explosion of innovation. New forms of presentation will emerge and wrap us in more news than we can constructively use: information glut to an unfathomed degree. We will be bombarded with news of the world, designed by us and, in turn, transmitted from us to others who will exponentially expand and distort our knowledge. The problem won't be access but filtering the torrents of news into byte-sized information we can use. Without gatekeepers, we will be swamped with a mixture of gems, muck, and mire.

Just as the big bang gave birth to our universe more than 13 billion years ago, the digital revolution is expanding our information universe. Innovators will continue to devise electronic nets to catch the information flying through space, and, as it is scooped up, other devices will process and organize it for our use. The information that we designate as "news" will be differentiated into a variety of forms and then delivered in the most timely and convenient of them. The media will be fast moving, portable, descriptive, textual, visual, and audible. It will be there when you want it and as you want it presented. And it will be up to you to decide its value and validity. The wise will not drown.

Index